First published in 1999 by the
BRITISH FILM INSTITUTE
21 Stephen Street, London W1P 2LN

The British Film Institute
promotes greater understanding and
appreciation of, and access to, film and
moving image culture in the UK.

British Library Cataloguing-in-Publication Data
A catalogue record for this book is available from the British Library

ISBN 0–85170–773–4

Series design by
Andrew Barron & Collis Clements Associates

Typeset in Fournier and Franklin Gothic by
D R Bungay Associates, Burghfield, Berks.

Printed in Great Britain by The Cromwell Press, Trowbridge, Wiltshire

CONTENTS

ACKNOWLEDGMENTS
. . . .

When Ed Buscombe asked me to take on this task it was because Lindsay Anderson, to whom it had originally been assigned, had died before he could tackle it. To say that I therefore approached the job with a profound sense of inadequacy is a gross understatement; but, on the other hand, having an opportunity unreservedly to praise a classic British documentary film-maker when I had spent no little time questioning the value of Grierson, the central figure of the British Documentary Film Movement, the rest of his circle and his legacy, was more than welcome. So here are some thoughts on *"Fire Were Started –"* (hereafter referred to more simply and conventionally as *Fires Were Started*) provoked by Lindsay Anderson (whose seminal essay on Jennings is here reprinted as an appendix and is the source of my chapter titles); by Dai Vaughan's great book on Jennings' film-editor Stewart McAllister (*Portrait of an Invisible Man*); by Jeffrey Richards' full account of the production and reception of the film in the book he wrote with Anthony Aldgate (*Britain Can Take It*); by the many others who have written about Jennings or made programmes about him; by my colleagues Vincent Porter and John Corner; by Andrew Lockett and Rob White of BFI Publishing; and by Ed Buscombe, of course. My text has been corrected by Vincent Porter and, as ever, my wife to neither of whom does any blame attach for errors and infelicities.

1

....

'A FRESH AND LOVING EYE'

In our city darkened now, street and square and crescent,
We can feel our living past in our shadowed present,
Ghosts beside our starlit Thames
Who lived and loved and died
Keep throughout the ages London Pride
Noël Coward, 'London Pride', Summer 1941

At one time I used to emerge from a showing of *Fires Were Started*
feeling the finest thing in the world was to be a member of the Auxiliary
Fire Service in 1941. Now I am more inclined to think that the finest
thing in the world (or at least in the English Cinema) was to have been
making a film about the A.F.S. in [1942].
Daniel Millar, *Sight and Sound*, Spring 1969

The reputation of Humphrey Jennings, alone among those of his fellows
in the British Documentary Film Movement of the 1930s and 40s,
remains unsullied and un-revised. Hence the appearance of his
masterpiece *Fires Were Started* in the BFI Archive list of the 360
indispensable films of the cinema's first eight decades.

Fires Were Started is the only representative of the British
documentary tradition in the list despite this body of work having once
been claimed, albeit by one of its own leading practitioners (Paul Rotha),
as 'a progressive, creative and continuous output of films that was the
envy of many other countries'. This neglect, though, is not to be
wondered at. Today, the classic pre-'fly-on-the-wall' documentaries are
ignored by audiences, who tend anyway not to classify them as
documentaries at all; their fate is to be endlessly picked over by
squabbling film scholars, who relentlessly dispute their worth and quality.
But in these obscure debates, almost without question, Jennings remains
above the fray.

Lindsay Anderson is the key here, via that seminal 1954 appraisal of
Jennings, reprinted below by way of afterword. It is the foundation upon
which received opinion about the Cambridge-educated painter, poet and
film-maker rests:

For reality, [Jennings'] wartime films stand alone; and they are sufficient achievement. They will last because they are true to their time, and because the depth of feeling in them can never fail to communicate itself. They will speak for us to posterity, saying: 'This is what it was like. This is what we were like – the best of us'.

Those who have shielded the flame of Jennings' reputation, all of whom follow in Anderson's footsteps, speak of this 'depth of feeling' arising from a wondrous ability to observe humanity authentically – what Anderson elsewhere called 'the extraordinary truth of his people'. This is the true distinguishing mark of the films and one of the foundations of the settled view of Jennings. Even those hostile to him, such as John Grierson himself, the founder of the Documentary Movement, for whom Jennings was never quite a team player, agreed. He wrote after Jennings' death that he 'was a rare one in our group, with qualities of style and observation all his own'. For the critic Dilys Powell these qualities meant that Jennings 'was happy conveying the feel of a human being: The way a man walks, shouts to his friends, the way a girl sings at her work.' Gavin Lambert echoed this view: '… glimpses of ordinary people … caught with such quick affection and precision, without trace of patronage or caricature.'

By the 80s, Stuart Hood could draw attention to the fact that Jennings was 'essentially conservative' without really denting his reputation. More typically, during that same period, Sir Roland Penrose, introducing a solo exhibition on Jennings' life and work as an artist and writer as well as a film-maker, talked of him as 'a genius of remarkable quality'. And the judgment of genius remains. In a radio tribute

'This is what it was like': fatigue at 14 Local Control

'Glimpses of ordinary people':
Mrs. Townsend pours tea after
the raid

celebrating Humphrey Jennings' place in the cinema's first century in 1995, Sir Denis Forman ranked him as such with Jean Vigo, despite the very few films each created:

> The evidence of [his genius] is slender but there is enough to make people recognise it and prick up their ears and say: 'Here walked somebody that had the power to move us beyond the way that most film directors can move us. He was a great man.'

And for many, *Fires Were Started*, Jennings' feature length documentary made at the official Crown Film Unit, about the work of the Auxiliary Fire Service (A.F.S.) during the 1940–41 London Blitz, is the masterwork. Lambert specifically cited it as the 'strongest' instant of this talent 'to make contact with all kinds of people, to present them naturally, acutely observed'. Anderson was to agree and, indeed, go further:

> No other British film made during the war, documentary or feature, achieved such a continuous and poignant truthfulness, or treated the subject of men at war with such a sense of its incidental glories and its essential tragedy.

It is (wrote Jim Hillier): 'Jennings' best, and most individualised, evocation of the personal qualities of ordinary people, their courage, their acceptance of other humans, their unquestioning and determined commitment to a group task.' At the end of the 60s, Daniel Millar was even more extravagant in his praise:

'The subject of men at war …
and its essential tragedy.'
Finding dead Jacko's helmet

Fires Were Started, now 26 years old, seems to me the highest achievement of British cinema; and Jennings is not only the greatest documentarist but also, counting Chaplin and Hitchcock as American, the greatest film-maker that this country has produced.

2

. . . .

'AN INTELLECTUAL ARTIST'

While that last judgment might be disputed, it is certainly the case that Humphrey Jennings was the most paradoxical of British film-makers. Jennings was a dilettante to many of his colleagues, but one with an obsessive compulsion for perfection. He was an artist who was, in the opinion of some, far too intellectual to be any such thing. (This seems to me to be a peculiarly English sort of formulation.) He was a surrealist who became an arch-realist. He was a great film-maker, but he had no particular time for film as an art form. He was a remarkable observer of his fellow humanity but was, by many accounts, something of a failure at his own personal and professional relationships. He was a great patriot who nevertheless sent his wife and children to America for the duration of the War. There is even an ambiguity about his tragic early death in 1950, aged forty-three, falling from a rock while recce-ing a shoot in Greece. Accident or suicide? It is perhaps apposite that the most human production still of Jennings shows him playfully balancing on a table on the *Fires Were Started* Recreation (Rec.) Room set.

Humphrey Jennings was born in Walberswick, Suffolk, on 19 August 1907 to a left-leaning architect and a sometime art student. He was sent to the rather progressive Perse School in Cambridge and thence to Pembroke College, Cambridge. At Perse he became interested in drama primarily as a designer, an interest he continued at university and after. He took a starred First in the English Tripos and began an academic career by securing a research bursary to study the poet Thomas Gray. This did not solidify into either a thesis or a university teaching position so, in conjunction with his scholarly inquiries, he became increasingly involved in a wide range of artistic and other activities. He taught school a little, painted, wrote, designed and edited. Eventually he was also occasionally to broadcast. Yet somehow, despite his talent at all or most of these things, none of these employments grew into a conventional full-time occupation.

As a result he was available for all sorts of fascinating odd jobs. He designed some silks for a firm in Paris. He was a key figure in mounting the first International Surrealist Exhibition in London. He dreamed up the Mass Observation project with a Cambridge friend, the poet and journalist Charles Madge and anthropologist Tom Harrisson. Meanwhile, as the 30s progressed, film in the form of the G.P.O. Film Unit under John Grierson, came to dominate, but not quite monopolise, his working life.

Jennings had a stereotypical upper middle-class English aspect, lanky and tweedy. According to Denis Forman, he dressed 'as an undergraduate would dress – tweed jacket and grey trousers – not the great artist'. That combination of fractured career and somewhat etiolated appearance is obviously one source for the mistaken impression of his being a dabbler. In fact there is no suggestion that he ever brought anything other than compulsive attention and professionalism to the task in hand. He had quite formidable energy levels especially during the Second World War when he, like his colleagues, would often be in the preliminary phase of research on one project while shooting another and supervising the final cut of a third. Overall he balanced a lack of commitment to a career path with an obsessive ability to focus down.

Nor did the fact that he was clever dispel the dilettante canard in a society prone to categorise really bright intellectuals who are not shy about their love of learning and debate as having (in our absurd current expression) 'two brains'. The nature of poetic language, the cutting edge of experiment in the plastic arts, the impact of industrialisation, an interest (before professional French historians came up with the concept) in *l'histoire des méntalités* – Jennings' agenda of concerns was perceived to be formidable and he was not hesitant in insisting that these topics ought to matter to those around him. Forman remembered that: 'He had an eye which would fix on his listeners ... and he would talk to us as a master.'

Some, Julian Trevelyan for instance, thought 'that Humphrey's intellect was too brilliant for a painter'; and if he weren't too clever for art in general, then even Anderson considered he might have been 'perhaps too intellectual for the cinema'. The general opinion among those involved in the Documentary Film Movement was that his ideas were always a jump or two ahead of what the medium could stand. Jennings reported to his wife, Cicely, that Paul Rotha had accused him of 'going religious' for using the 'Hallelujah Chorus' at the end of the early wartime short *This is England*. (Anderson, on the contrary, thought this sequence which cross-cut the ruins of Coventry cathedral and an aircraft factory against the singing, 'extraordinary' and the moment when Jennings found 'his style'.) A year later, Edgar Anstey savaged *Listen to Britain* in *The Spectator* calling it 'the rarest piece of fiddling since the days of Nero. It will be a disaster if this film is sent overseas. One shudders to think the effect upon our allies.'

(Anstey was to learn, from his wife who was in the States, that the film was a success there. And this appears to have been the general opinion, leading Jennings to write to Cicely, also in America at that time, that it 'shows it's worth taking the trouble and not underrating people'.) But basically they seemed to have thought of him as, to use Harry Watt's description, 'a skinny, chinless fawn'.

Jennings returned the compliment, writing of 'Rotha and other Grierson's little boys' whose talk of '"pure documentary" and "realism" was nothing more than "self-advertisement"'. They might have thought him condescending and pretentious but he saw them in the same way as 'grubby documentary boys who try and give a hand to what they call emerging humanity, the common man and so on'.

One source of tension had to be that, unlike his colleagues, Jennings did not make politics and economics a central concern. Even the War did not stop him thinking 'that the real world is the world of Uccello and Mozart', although he too was left-wing by background and inclination. For example, he noted how the long period of disinformation about the

Soviet Union was having to be reversed given 'the simple fact of Russian resistance': 'As for the Russians our enthusiasm is nobody's business.'

In retrospect, it is clear that Jennings did not acknowledge the divide between his intellectual interests and his artistic work. This was because, as Dai Vaughan has observed, 'He really didn't belong in the world of English art at all. His sensibility was continental'; and in the rest of Europe's mental landscape the Anglophone chasm between theory and practice is less acknowledged, if it is deemed to exist at all. Jennings' entire career constitutes a 'continental' (as it might be) refutation of an English assumption that 'intellectual artist' is something of an oxymoron. He balanced the two elements effortlessly because he was simply unaware of the need so to do; the intellectual pyrotechnics of his films remain a major source of their continued fascination.

That such a figure was generally disdainful of the cinema is less of a mystery. No intelligentsia (except perhaps the American) was more hostile to the popular art of the cinema than was the British. No artistic community was less interested in exploiting film as a medium of expression than the British. The pre-war cinematic avant-garde was almost entirely overtly politically driven, its artistic agenda attenuated. It is often said that Jennings turned to film only because he needed a wage. In 1929, the year of his graduation, he married Cicely Cooper, the daughter of a very senior railway engineer. In 1933 Mary-Lou, the first of his two daughters, was born. A year later he was hanging around the G.P.O. doing some designing, directing and editing. There was enough going on there for him to move the family from 19a British Grove, Hammersmith, his first London home, to Blackheath where the studios were. But that did not imply a commitment to the new art. Cicely averred that he took a cynical view – film was simply a way to make money.

This has always sounded a little pat to me. Certainly, Jennings' finances were of an opaque English upper middle-class kind; but Grierson was not normally seen as a source of largesse. His supposed radicalism did not stretch to embracing the unionisation of his own shop, for example; and he was notorious for the low wages he paid – postman rather than film technician rates – to his middle-class colleagues, who could presumably work for him and remain middle-class only because they could afford to do so through private means. For Jennings, who was able to send his family to America for the duration of the War, achieving a conventional flow of revenue simply does not seem to have been a permanent or crippling priority, although Kevin Jackson, editor of *The Humphrey Jennings Film Reader*, states that his letters to Cicely do document 'chronic financial worries'.

Perhaps finance was suggested as the imperative which drove him into film work because it in some way justifies his disdain for cinema as an art form. Mary-Lou said in 1970: 'I don't think he liked films at all – I think he was a bit ashamed of it, you know, it wasn't really culture.' This sounds simply as if he was not able to rise above the general prejudices of his class at that time, or above the specific hostility of the Documentary Movement towards the commercial cinema. Grierson, who had been a very effective film critic in the 20s, came to fulminate constantly against mainstream movies not least, I believe, because as a documentarist he was losing the battle for audience against them. The industry returned the compliment. A satiric piece in the technician union's (A.C.T.) journal suggested that the aspirant documentarist must: 'A) Be a gentleman: B) Be a socialist: C) Have had a Varsity education D) Have a private income' and even 'H) Have an adenoidal expression' (cf.: Humphrey Jennings?).

This animosity from the trade as well as from his colleagues did not prevent Jennings pushing the limits of the medium. On the contrary, by applying some of his intellectual insights to his own film work, Jennings easily balanced his specific personal experimental project against a general snobbish view of the cinema as a social phenomenon. He certainly began learning film technique enthusiastically enough, writing to Cicely after his first day at the G.P.O. in Blackheath that 'it is very exhilarating stuff'.

The clue to balancing surrealism and realism lies in his involvement with Mass Observation. He, Madge and Harrisson, who had just returned from field work in the New Hebrides, conceived the project at the end of 1936, some six months after the Surrealist Exhibition. For Kathleen Raine, another Cambridge friend, surrealism led to Mass Observation because they both had a bearing on 'Humphrey's interest in the collective imagination and its expression'. There is also a further association in that the sociological notions underpinning Mass Observation often produced surreal agendas for inquiry. It has been noted more than once that the list of the things in which Mass Observation was interested, as itemised in the *New Statesman* letter from Jennings, Madge and Harrisson announcing the formation of the group, could be read as a surrealist poem:

A horse in the raid – the surrealism of the blitz

Shouts and gestures of motorists
The aspidistra cult
Anthropology of football pools
Bathroom behaviour
Beards, armpits, eyebrows...
Funerals and Undertakers
Female taboos about eating
The private lives of midwives

The move from fine art to social science is, therefore, perhaps more logical and much less dilettanteish than it might first appear.

In turn, the move from Mass Observation to the documentary film is not much of a jump at all. Jennings and Madge wrote up a massive report of the major Mass Observation exercise undertaken on 12 May 1937, George VI's Coronation Day when observers all over the country attempted to document responses to the event. Stuart Legg, Jennings' closest friend at the G.P.O. Film Unit and the man who had introduced him to Grierson, believed that *May the Twelfth* with its positively surrealist montage of observation, quotations from ordinary people and citations from literature was the origin of Jennings' attempts to create films which also reflected such diversity and simultaneity.

Less positively, one can also detect the influence of Mass Observation in a quality of detached, even cynical, observation which can be read into some of the films, notably the study of popular leisure activities, *Spare Time*, which was Jennings' major solo directing effort prior to the War. Mass Observation's interest in people turned them into scientific objects of inquiry and there is no necessary connection between the observer and the subject. Such a disconnection gives rise to the whiffs of condescension which some see in this film, the sort of thing that led Grierson on one occasion to suggest to Forman that they might care to go to the cutting room to 'see Humphrey being nice to the common people'. Whether Jennings was contemptuous of the people he filmed or of the system which so impoverished their circumstances remains at best ambiguous. It is clear, though, that all G.P.O./Documentary Movement films shared with the sociological enterprise a desire to document the everyday, to offer pictures of typical aspects of British life.

The paradox that Jennings was such a good observer of people while being less than effective at his own interpersonal relationships is more difficult to resolve than these other balancing acts. Robert Vas, himself a distinguished documentarist and, therefore, like many of his colleagues much influenced by Jennings (albeit in rather indirect ways), made a portrait film of the man for the BBC arts programme *Omnibus* in 1970, whence many of the interviews I quote. It is unexpectedly revealing. Against the then conventional wisdom that, *pace Spare Time*, Jennings loved people because otherwise he could not have got those wonderfully revealing shots upon which his reputation rests, we find Mary-Lou stating: 'I don't think he was really aware of people at all. I don't think he understood about them. It was part of his nature.' Her younger sister, Charlotte, in effect glosses 'people' to include herself: 'Did I have a father? No!'

The Jennings family had (in the phrase of the day) 'gone with the wind up' to the States, leaving Dad behind to become, paradoxically, the country's most effective patriotic advocate on film. As even the Royal Family, whose princesses were only a few years older than the Jennings girls, stayed put, this is as hard to understand as his finances. Cicely Jennings, in her interview with Vas, regretted Humphrey's persistent absences of which the war-time separation was merely the longest. She saw his early death as simply the last and most irrevocable of this series.

Despite these negatives, there is also consistent contrary testimony that he was a man of considerable vitality and charisma, qualities that were somehow transformed into an acute ability to empathise with those outside his circle with whom he found himself working on the films. He had considerable leadership qualities and, according to Mary Lou, was 'a terrific extrovert' with 'a wonderful sense of humour'. The writer William Sansom, who was also a volunteer auxiliary fireman and appeared in *Fires Were Started*, recalled that during filming Jennings 'dealt well. Democracy the rule, Christian names all round, discussion and beer together after work – he gave us the sense of making the film *with* him instead of *for* him.'

Perhaps this paradox of the unfeeling but empathetic Jennings can only be resolved by suggesting that it was the camera and the War which together furnished him with the wherewithal he needed to understand his fellow creatures. It is certainly not the camera alone, because *Spare Time* conspicuously lacks the warmth of the later efforts. Only when the War comes does the camera facilitate a sympathetic vision of people, at last allowing Jennings to interact with them to obtain what Dai Vaughan called the 'strangely memorable' shots of the great films. Lindsay Anderson: 'It is as if this detached somewhat theoretical Cambridge intellectual suddenly found his imagination warmed to life by the hot blast of war. Emotion became a possibility.'

No task did more to effect this transformation than the making of *Fires Were Started*, as Jennings himself admitted to Cicely in a letter written in April 1942 during the shoot:

> it has now become 14 hours a day – living in Stepney the whole time – really have never worked so hard at anything or I think thrown myself into anything so completely. Whatever the results it is definitely an advance in film making for me – really beginning to understand people and not just looking at them and lecturing or pitying them. Another general effect of the war. Also should make me personally more bearable.

But let us not go too far.

Film directors often seem to have an 'I'm the king of the world' approach to their business and Jennings was no exception. Sansom recalled that all the firemen and the film crew, including Jennings, were burned during the shoot. Sansom also remembered that Jennings 'shouted awesomely, and often smiled – but with the quick fade of one who really has no time for it'.

I have already indicated disagreements with his fellow documentary directors and, as C. Pennington-Richards, the cameraman

All the firemen and film crew
were burned during the shoot

on *Fires Were Started*, confirmed, he was just as much at odds with
Stewart McAllister, his editor and closest collaborator, with whom he had
constant 'volcanic' arguments. Jenny Stein (née Hutt), McAllister's
assistant who went on to edit *A Diary for Timothy*, the other Jennings'
masterwork, told Vaughan that: 'They had this sort of – joke – love-hate
relationship and they were always shouting and screaming at each other.'
Francis Cockburn, one of the production assistants on *Fires Were Started*,
recalled that McAllister 'and Humphrey were inseparable. ... I think it
would be true to call them friends, though Humphrey was a very
detached sort of person.' They were exceptionally paranoid about each
changing the film behind the other's back, an especially important source
of anxiety for men who would spend days arguing about trimming or
adding two frames from or to a shot.

Jennings regularly terrorised his crews. Joe Mendoza worked on
Listen to Britain:

> He had a tremendous reputation for working assistant directors –
> sort of having nervous breakdowns on him two-at-a-time on every
> movie ... and I begged the production manager not to make me
> work on the film. ... And so she said to me, 'Well look, he is very
> difficult to handle because everybody is frightened of him.'

Nora Lee (née Dawson), Jennings' assistant director on *Fires Were
Started* (but with the screen credit 'Unit Manager'), recalled for Vas a
Jennings who jumped all over the warehouse roof location looking for
shots: 'And if he had been particularly tiresome during the day, the rather

ghoulish unit would sit around and say, "That's right! Just about six inches further back, Humphrey."'

What is really ghoulish about this memory of Jennings is that Nora Lee still feels able to tell it to camera decades later despite the fact that the man died in exactly this way, falling from a great height. He was killed on the island of Poros on 24 September 1950, while setting up a documentary on Europe's health to be called *The Good Life*. Doubts about the accidental nature of Jennings' death seem to turn generally on the thought that, after having such a 'good war', he had been reduced to making films with titles like *The Dim Little Island*. Stuart Legg suggested it could have been 'an unconscious suicide', but this seems far-fetched. There is no indication of a desire for death, or even of depression. His last letter home was very upbeat: '... except for a little toothache I feel fine'. Moreover, Lee's anecdote, which is also supported by Tom Harrisson's memories, is evidence that Jennings could become so absorbed in framing a shot (or perhaps sketching it) that he could easily have lost his footing and stepped backwards into space. His wife, Cicely, believed he had done no such thing but, rather, had fractured his skull in a lesser fall after grasping at loose rock.

There does remain the question of coincidence. After all, this was Britain's most effective patriotic film-maker whose first London home just happened to be in a street called British Grove. Harrisson remarked that, 'He was a person who liked *wild* ideas. He believed for instance that coincidence is one of the keys to human behaviour. He was always looking for coincidence.' So the fact that he was carrying a copy of Trelawney's *Last Days of Shelley and Byron* at the time of his death was bound to loom large. His producer, Ian Dalrymple, made much of the fact:

This is the sort of coincidence Humphrey was always coming upon in his researches. Once when he went to shoot a cargo ship for a symbolic purpose, he discovered, to his joy and amazement, that her name was BRITISH GENIUS. He rang me up from the North with huge satisfaction just to tell me. I said, "Oh! Humphrey, you do have the luck." But he didn't think it was luck, or coincidence; it was the truth that won't be denied. Things like that were always happening to him and now this last has. And I don't think that was coincidence either. I just think Greece has claimed another English poet.

3
....
'THE SIMPLEST OF PICTURES'

Coincidence, happenstance – much less casual observational filming – actually play very little, if any, part in Jennings' documentary film-making method. The G.P.O. Film Unit evolved an approach, especially after the coming of synch sound in the early 1930s, which required extremely extensive and careful research and pre-filming preparation along the same lines demanded by a fiction film. Not for them, Jennings included, today's point-and-shoot documentary encounters, where research often seems to be nothing more than obtaining permission to film and the rest, supposedly, just 'happens'.

Documentarists in this pre-'fly-on-the-wall' era nevertheless felt themselves to be constrained in ways that fiction film-makers were not. They needed to legitimise their scripts or treatments by tying them to this complex process of research. Harry Watt, for example, went through some 3,000 flight reports while preparing the first of the war-time documentary features, *Target for Tonight*. In addition he spent time in top-secret locations such as Bomber Command and lived on an R.A.F. base at Mildenhall.

If the topic were general enough, the Blitz for example, film-makers could rely on their own memory. They felt able to use accounts of other eye-witnesses as a basis for scenes and dialogue. Finally, and most importantly, they could (as Watt did) also write up events, dialogue or situations which they themselves had observed during a specific research period. What they avoided, or implied they avoided, was imagination. Behind everything they filmed – however much scripted, however often rehearsed, however many the takes – was a prior witnessed reality. The claim on the real in these circumstances was not that the camera filmed things as they were happening, but that it filmed things as they had happened and been witnessed.

In January 1941, the Public Relations Committee of the Civil Defence had suggested that a drama emphasising teamwork and fire-fighting was an obvious way of realising this aim. The first phase of the Blitz had begun on 5 September 1940 and ended with a raid against London on 10 May 1941. The pre-war system of autonomous fire brigades, augmented after 1938 by the A.F.S., had been stretched to breaking point and an integrated National Fire Service was established in response in autumn 1941. Despite these difficulties, though, the first phase of the Blitz failed. It had destroyed much property but had not broken morale and could therefore be turned to good propaganda account. That one of the characters should die was deemed intrinsic to the project by the Ministry of Information (MoI); it was vital to demonstrate that sacrifice was necessary. Thus a note that one of the firemen was 'going to get killed' is in Jennings' earliest plans for the film.

'Gimme that life line': Jacko's fatal decision

When the Crown Film Unit (which is what, within the MoI, Grierson's old G.P.O. Film Unit had become in summer 1940) took up the proposal, Harry Watt suggested to Ian Dalrymple, the unit's producer[1], that Jennings might be the man for the job. Since Jennings was generally regarded, not least by Watt, as an intellectual who had never escaped his painterly background to master the art of documentary narrative, it is hard to see why he should have been proposed for a long re-enacted film, in effect a conventional story, if not to entrap him (and Dalrymple whom Watt also disliked) into some sort of disaster.

Dalrymple, on the other hand, had the highest regard for Jennings. He got on with him so well that, after Jennings' London digs narrowly escaped destruction during the Blitz, he invited Jennings to lodge at his own house in Chorley Wood in exurban Hertfordshire. Jennings took on the 'N.F.S. Film' (although in the event *Fires Were Started* does not actually portray the integrated N.F.S. but rather the prior, more complicated situation).

Fires Were Started was never for a moment subjected to the flood of ideas for *mélange* and montage which marks Jennings' surviving written thoughts on, and plans for, the earlier films. Jennings might have been seen as an experimentalist, but from the outset on this film he had a clear and straightforwardly conventional vision of its structure. All the documents he prepared in the run-up to principal photography on *Fires Were Started* demonstrate a sure grasp of standard narrative form, slowly fleshing out research notes into outlines and eventually producing in the 'Fifth Treatment' a script, albeit one idiosyncratically laid out and often oscillating back into synopsis form. In a letter to Cicely dated 11 January 1941 he was already describing this document as 'a detailed script of the fire film' and, even if it was not quite what any mainstream studio would acknowledge as a script, it was certainly far more detailed than any of the pre-production working notes he usually produced. The less conventional films never had scripts at all; they relied instead on often quite full but always impressionistic treatments, which caused Dalrymple considerable difficulties with the men at the Ministry and others.

Jennings had been at work on the 'fire film' since September 1941. Over that autumn and early winter he accumulated a considerable amount of research material, but the shape of the film actually did not change that much. The biggest development was that some factory women whom Jennings first thought of as the element to be threatened by the blaze gave place to the munitions ship which has the same function in the story as filmed. Otherwise the basic structure remained constant – an exposition to introduce the firemen and women and the fire service in general, followed by a climatic fire – an 'average occurrence' – which was to claim the life of one of the men. This structure divides into the seven sequences of the film as Jennings and McAllister finished it.

The exposition takes three sequences. The film begins as a Heavy Unit (H.U.) fire engine is being driven back to Substation Y of Fire Station 14. Jacko, an A.F.S. fireman, says goodbye to his wife at their newspaper shop. Another A.F.S. man, Johnny, stops boxing in the garden with his young son and also leaves for duty. The rest of the men whom we will come to know as the crew of H.U.1 are caught simply walking to the school which has been converted into their substation. In conversations, the dangers of a promised full moon and the news of the munitions ship berthed at a dock within the substation's 'ground' are raised. A new A.F.S. fireman, Barrett, following directions from a local Chinese man, arrives and provides the pretence for formal introductions to the crew. Life at the station goes on – everyday chores from peeling potatoes to cleaning the appliances – and the next level of organisation at the main station, 14 Local Control, is introduced.

Segue to the second sequence which illustrates the structure of the fire service more generally. Now no attempt is made to name or individualise the people seen, although the women and their male supervisors at 14 Local Control will appear again later. The sequence begins with 14 Local Control asking the firewomen (W.A.F.S., Women's Auxiliary Fire Service) on duty at 14Y, Mrs Townsend (Mrs T.) and Betty Martin, for their 'return of appliances'. Local Control continues this routine by calling all its substations to obtain a full picture of 14's strength, at the same time giving us, the audience, more of the service's jargon. Jennings' notes explain that: 'During and leading from this dictation, a "documentary" sequence of men and appliances' follows. We see training and the preparations of a fire boat (where the difficulty of operating at low tide is planted). This second sequence, which most closely accords with the norms of a public education documentary, as Jennings' use of the term 'documentary' (in quotes) indicates, concludes with the strong image of two firemen atop turntable ladders (T.T.L.s) being raised up against the sky.

Meanwhile (as it were) back at 14Y it is now lunchtime. In the third expository sequence, Sub-Officer (S/O) Dykes, the regular London Fire Brigade (L.F.B.) man and 'headmaster' of 14Y, suggests to Johnny that, after lunch, he take Barrett round the station's 'ground'. More of the back-story is now revealed. A sunken barge, an emergency source of water, is inspected and the paradox of how hard it is to find water for fire-fighting despite being next to the river is explained. Johnny shows Barrett the munitions ship at Alderman's Wharf. Nearby Trinidad Street, which will be the site of the fire, is also introduced.

Exposition over, the next three sequences deal with the 'average occurrence' of a raid and the fires it starts. This fourth sequence, designated in one draft as 'Before Battle', is set in the afternoon and early evening lull before the raid. It doesn't advance the action much but simply revisits the men introduced in the first sequence, using their expectant wait for nightfall to flesh out their characters. In their billet, known as the 'Monkey House', the crew sleeps. Johnny wakes Jacko by throwing a paper ball at him and tea is brewed. In brigade headquarters, the Commanding Officer confirms that there will be a raid. In the Rec. Room, the firemen play snooker, table-tennis or darts and the black-out is put up. The bar is open. B.A., the crew's comedian, tries to sell new man Barrett some braces. The arms ship is reintroduced. At Observation Post (O.P.) Control a strong wind is reported. Back at 14Y, the team now gathers as Barrett, on the piano, plays them into the Rec. with the old folk song, 'One Man Went to Mow'. The siren warning of the air-raid sounds. Rumbold, the intellectual of the group and nicknamed the 'Colonel', reads an extract from Sir Walter Raleigh on the nature of death.

The Trinidad Street warehouse fire constitutes the fifth sequence of the film, designated as 'attack' and 'counterattack'. An observation post (O.P.) on the other side of the river reports that incendiary bombs are falling to its central O.P. Control. The 'counterattack' begins with H.U.1 and our crew leaving 14Y for the warehouse. They arrive to discover fire on the top floor. There is a danger of 'explosions at the fire'; because of this and the proximity of the munitions ship at Alderman's Wharf, Dykes calls for more appliances. Two hoses ('branches') are connected to a hydrant and a fire boat is dispatched by District Control although, as the tide is out, it will not be of much use. A District Officer (D/O) is also sent to Trinidad Street.

The crew is failing to contain the fire, a fact noted by the Greek chorus in the O.P. The water supply from the hydrant gives out and the men move to obtain a replacement supply from the sunken barge. Scenes at Local, District and Brigade Control make us aware that the raid is extensive and the service is becoming stretched. The District Officer arrives with reinforcement trailer pumps (T.P.s). 14 Control sustains a

The Greek chorus in the
Observation Post

close hit and one of the firewomen is slightly injured. The extra T.P.s pump the water from the sunken barge to the branches at the fire. On the warehouse roof, Dykes cannot make contact with the ground, so sends Rumbold down a burning staircase to explain his situation. The D/O sends Barrett back to the roof to tell Dykes a turntable ladder unit is coming. The stairwell is engulfed with flames.

Dykes is injured but the T.T.L. arrives to rescue him. This is the climax of the film. The unconscious Dykes is winched down, a process

Dykes is injured

which requires the holding of a lifeline on the roof. Jacko insists on doing this and Barrett unwillingly goes down the T.T.L., leaving Jacko alone. Jacko's foot is engulfed by flame. As he falls there is a huge explosion.

In the sixth sequence, entitled 'Came the dawn', the 'all clear' sounds and a mobile canteen arrives at Trinidad Street. The men begin 'knocking-off' and 'making up', turning off the water and clearing the site. A unit from sixty miles away finally finds 14Y. Dykes is in hospital with a head injury; back at the fire making up continues. The O.P. phones O.P. Control to say that they think the fire appears to be contained. Jacko's helmet is found. The munitions ship is undamaged. In Jacko's newspaper shop, his 'widow' hears on the radio that '... fires were started –' Meanwhile the loading of munitions continues. The crew of H.U.1 are back at the 'Monkey House'. Rumbold reads a passage from Shakespeare which serves as an obituary for Jacko. B.A. tells them to snap out of their mood.

Finally there is a short coda. This takes place two days later, according to the 'Fifth Treatment', cross-cutting Jacko's funeral with the departure of the munitions ship. As Jacko is laid to rest, the ship's bow ploughs through the water. The film ends.

Despite the distinction drawn between the second 'documentary' sequence and the rest of the film, the supposition is that all the events in this narrative, including the dialogue, had occurred in one circumstance or another; in effect, that nothing had been 'made up'. And it is possible to source much of the film in prior realities.

Jennings obviously used his own experience of the Blitz as a starting point. He had made much in his letters to Cicely of what a transformative event he thought it was for the whole society: 'What warmth – what courage! What determination.' Beyond giving him a clear idea of the atmosphere he wanted to create, such memories also inspired *Fires Were Started* more directly. For example, a line from *I See*

Jacko's 'widow' hears on the radio that '… fires were started –'

Jacko is laid to rest

'A one-legged man crossing the fire'

London, a poem he wrote in May 1941 as a clear response to the actual sights of the Blitz, becomes one of the film's more memorable images a year later:

I see a one-legged man crossing the fire on crutches... [2]

There is similar 'authority' (if you will) for the sing-song in the fourth sequence. In October 1941, Jennings was in Liverpool interviewing John Lappin, an A.F.S. man who had won a medal for gallantry during the Blitz. While there Jennings had heard, and then made a note about, people 'singing in the public shelters: "One man went to mow – went to mow a meadow."'

He also had other people's memories and research efforts to hand. For example, there is an apparently unsolicited letter dated 6 February 1941 from a Rosamund Davies. This contained a proposal for 'Episodes in the Life of an Ambulance Driver'. Among other things she confirms that 'after a meal in the canteen we would frequently hold a sing-song'. Less randomly, Maurice Richardson, an A.F.S. man credited with 'story collaboration' on the film, provided many pages of observation and snatches of dialogue. Here is Richardson's note and the same dialogue as it appears in the film:

RICHARDSON	FIRES WERE STARTED
S / O: 'Is this Y14?'	S / O: 'Is this Y14?'
MRS T.: 'That's right.'	MRS T.: 'Yes.'

S/O: 'Thank the Lord for that. We've had an awful job finding your place.'

MRS T.: 'Who are you?'
S/O: 'T.P. No. 5. Abbotsden's F.S. We were sent here from your control to stand by.'
MRS T.: 'Abbotsden?'

S/O: 'The other side of Coleford.'

MRS T.: 'Why that's sixty miles away.'

S/O: ' We've had an awful job finding your place. We've come from Abbotsden. We were sent here from your control to stand by.'
MRS T.: 'Abbotsden?'
S/O: 'The other side of Coleford.'

MRS T.: 'Why that's sixty miles away.'
S/O: 'And don't I know it! You people seem to have taken a regular pasting down here tonight.'
MRS T.: 'Yes our boys are down at the docks.'

Jennings' specific researches included much time spent in various fire-stations around London. It was during a visit to Woolwich, for example, that he picked up a detailed account of the devastating raid on the Arsenal which occurred on 10 September 1940, and used one incident to produce a scene which seems at first sight to be much too good to be truly grounded in reality. During the film's climatic fire, a W.A.F.S. in 14 Control is on the phone to District Control as a nearby bomb shakes the station. She dives under the desk but reappears a moment later with a minor cut on her forehead and says, 'Control … Control … Control. Oh yes, sorry to be interrupted. We have another message for … .' This

'Control … Control. Oh yes, sorry to be interrupted'

image of the unfazed firewoman was so familiar during the War that it was being cartooned. One contemporary drawing has a dishevelled fireman in the midst of rubble saying to the pert operator whose switchboard is unscathed: 'I don't wish to interrupt, Dorothy – but I suppose you know that this station isn't standing anymore.' For all that it was a cliché of the day, the incident was duly recorded as an actual occurrence on page 2 of Jennings' typed-up notes.

In November, Jennings spent time at the Chelsea substation 6W. These repeated visits familiarised him with the normal routine of both stations and substations and with the overall structure of the pre-N.F.S. service, which had only just been abandoned. He heard stories (e.g. that when 6W had nearly been bombed, all the lights went out but the W.A.F.S. continued to work by candlelight) and saw routines (e.g. that all equipment was cleaned in the morning), some of which were to find a place in the film. This search for authentic incident continued throughout the shoot. For example, a penny-whistle player, whose haunting melody is heard in the first sequence as the men head for 14Y, seems like another typical and slightly surreal Jennings' invention. Yet it is no such thing. The man was playing one morning near the square where they were shooting and was, according to Sansom, 'instantly co-opted'.

In the last days of January 1942, Jennings finished the script/ treatment. He then turned to the logistics of shooting – props, locations and casting. 'The use of water during shooting will count as a fire drill so that no expense will be incurred.' This was no small matter since there were rows between the municipalities, the fire brigades and central government over who was to pay for the costs of responding to

The 'instantly co-opted' penny-whistle player

the Blitz, including bills for water. By 17 February, arrangements had been made for the loan of fire-fighting equipment: the H.U., a fire float, a turntable ladder, an ambulance, an auxiliary towing taxi, five trailer pumps and one mobile canteen. Impressive though this was, the equipment was actually inadequate to cope with the fires that Jennings set. The ebullient Fred Griffiths, who played 'Johnny' in the film, recalled for Vas that:

> Humphrey used to set the building alight so much that he had the Fire Brigade down there five or six times. You know, the real firemen. We had the appliances and we were real firemen but we never had the gear to put it out. And it caused a bit of animosity down there.

'Down there' was St Katharine's Docks.[3] As long as the river was involved, Jennings seems to have had a comparatively open mind about locations, adding, for example, a pencil note to his typed report on the November Chelsea visit that at No. 6. Brompton 'very good double garage doors open out on to pleasant square'. However, it is not difficult to understand why the film was finally located in the East End. Sacrificing a life to defend the mansions of Chelsea, or even the riverside factories of Lots Road, would not have had the same propaganda punch as Jennings obtained from setting the action in the heart of the East End – Wapping Church ('mentioned by Pepys', as he noted), the warehouse in St Katharine's Dock and Substation 14Y, housed in a primary school in Wellhouse Square.

Jennings had also been making notes on possible cast members during his research visits. Again this was common practice. Pat Jackson, having spent months at sea, cast *Western Approaches* by sitting in a Liverpool pub near the Shipping Federation and buying drinks for likely looking seamen. After three weeks he took no fewer than forty men down to Pinewood for tests. Jennings seemed to think that firemen already committed to performance, as evidenced by their participation in a 'Revue', might do. He met with the producer of the Revue and imagined 'the firemen climbing out of their ballet skirts – and going straight out to fight the biggest fire in history'. But this surreal thought was not pursued, perhaps because the revue was scheduled for the spring of 1942, exactly when Jennings was supposed to shoot.

Instead, Jennings seems to have picked up the cast from his recces, no fewer than four of them from the rejected Chelsea location. At Substation 6W, he had noticed some friezes by a Scottish sculptor Loris Rey in the recreation room. Like Stewart McAllister, Rey was a graduate of the Glasgow School of Art. He was to become 'Rumbold'. Fred Griffiths ('Johnny') was also at 6W with T. P. Smith ('B.A.') and John Barker ('Joe Vallance'). Jennings was still looking for the Sub-Officer in mid-February although he had found 'Jacko', Johnny Houghton of 28K, and Leading Fireman Philip Wilson-Dickson – 'Section Officer Walters'. 'Barrett', whose real name Sansom was incorrectly typed as 'Stantion', had also been cast from 13Y. 'Mrs Townsend', the senior W.A.F.S. at 14Y, was played by Assistant Group Officer Green. A regular fireman, Commanding Officer George Gravett, was eventually cast as 'Sub-Officer (S/O) Dykes'.

Why Jennings chose to use these fictitious names is quite hard to understand. There could have been little security reason for it and some of the cast did retain their own names: the more junior W.A.F.S. at 14Y, for example, are really called Betty and Eileen (Betty Martin and Eileen White). Moreover, not only names but jobs were also sometimes fictionalised. So while 'Johnny' (Fred Griffiths) was actually the one-time taxi-driver he says he was in the film,[4] 'Barrett', supposedly an advertising copywriter, was an author. On the other hand, 'Walters' (Wilson-Dickson) had worked in an advertising agency before the War. Changing the names meant losing the Wilson-Dickson hyphen; and Rey, Sansom and Gravett were replaced with 'Jacko' and 'Johnny' and other names with working-class resonances. Vincent Porter suggests that these false names help Jennings deliver a paean to class-less 'team-work' better to fulfil the MoI's original remit. The film as a whole celebrates collective endeavour and solidarity and, although Jacko 'dies', he is not the hero. The hero is without question the crew of H.U.1 rather than any individual.

Invented locations are easier to explain. No clue could be given which might reveal the pattern of fire service re-enforcement, so the latecomers arrive from a non-existent Abbotsden. The only Colefords in England are all in the West Country, far more than sixty miles from the London Docks. (In the same spirit, Harry Watt doubled the number of squadrons the RAF actually had for the charts on the walls of the huge Bomber Command set he built at Denham. 'We cheated,' said Watt.)

Principal photography, which should have begun on 5 February 1942, was a couple of weeks late and was to be a protracted business. Jennings spent six weeks shooting the fire alone, yielding what must be the most recycled, however much reconstructed, images of the Blitz ever made. The interiors were shot on sets at Pinewood designed by Edward ('Teddy') Carrick, who had worked on *Target for Tonight*. He was assisted by Loris Rey. The original schedule called for principal photography to be completed by 2 May but, although Jennings reported to Cicely on 29 May that, 'We are at last getting to the end of shooting the fire picture', filming continued into July.

All this points towards a conventional fictional film production – the script, the invented names, the sets – despite the legitimations provided by the documentary evidence arising from Jennings' extensive research. But Jennings was far from conventional in his approach to the shooting, which is perhaps one reason why it took so long. He sought to obtain an observational spontaneity by ad-libbing the scenes, even though he had dialogue available. Nora Lee recalls him giving her one sheet of paper and saying: 'And that is all the script they're getting, mate!' Not 'all the script there is', note; but rather, all that he was prepared to share. The cast therefore believed, in the words of William Sansom, that there was:

> No script. A general scheme, of course, which we did not know about. The film was shot both on and off the cuff. Dialogue was always made up on the spot – and of course the more genuine for that – and Jennings collected details of all kinds on the way, on the day, on the spot.

If so, then Jennings would be pretending to offer the dialogue that appeared in the Fifth Draft or in Maurice Richardson's additional notes as the spontaneous thought of the moment.

Jennings also seems to have induced deliberate exhaustion among his actors as a specific technique for directing the undemonstrative English. Wooden performances, especially when synch speech was required, were one of the banes of the classic documentary – the specific reason why many of these films 'died' in the 1930s. As well as hiding the script, Jennings apparently overcame this problem by simply repeating takes until people forgot their awkwardness or shyness. Take the most artificial of all the moments in *Fires Were Started*. Barrett is at the piano. As the men come down into the Rec. from the 'Monkey House', he and Johnny start to sing the old folk song 'One Man Went to Mow', which Jennings had heard about people singing on his trip to Liverpool. He made the firemen sing it all day. Fred Griffiths:

'I've started at half past eight in the morning': Johnny sings 'One Man Went to Mow'

I've started at half past eight in the morning and we go on singing all the way through. A break – half an hour, forty minutes for lunch. Start again. At 5 o'clock – cut! He [Jennings] comes over to me, he says: 'I think your voice is going.' I'd been singing for 9 hours and he said: 'Your voice is going.'

There are almost no moments of uneasiness in *Fires Were Started*. In the dawn sequence B.A.'s 'He's copped it, I tell you', when asked where Jacko is, is the worst. The *Documentary News Letter*, which was the mouthpiece of mainstream documentary opinion and as such by no means automatically enamoured of Jennings, said *Fires Were Started* presented on the screen 'the best handling of people on and off the job that we've seen in any British film' and 'maybe for the first time – proper working class dialogue'. This judgment remains exactly right. Somehow this tall, gangling, arrogant, cerebral director managed to facilitate the transfer of everyday behaviour through re-enactment, past the studio bulk of the equipment, on to the screen in a more or less pristine condition. Securing this account of 'what we were like' in such circumstances was, and remains, a remarkable achievement.

4

....

'THE IDEA OF CONNECTION'

In the first instance, Jennings' achievement is firmly centred on 'the extraordinary truth of his people'. The 'quick', 'acute' observation of 'the feel of a human being' was mainly created by the aggregation of discrete individual shots – images which Dai Vaughan described as having a 'strangely memorable quality': 'I say "strangely" because most of these shots are not at all cinematically ambitious. Typically they are routine cutaways. How, then do they achieve such a hold upon the mind?' Vaughan, with his film editor's keen eye, suggested it is because in these shots Jennings' subjects 'demonstrate albeit fleetingly, their awareness of the camera'.

> And my own experience tells me that, a frame or two after, they will have succeeded in composing themselves into that expression of earnest attentiveness or subdued yet eager endeavour for which the camera-operator habitually, professionally, waits. ... What we have [in Jennings' films] are segments balanced to a hairsbreadth between their contribution to the film and their affirmation of the subjects' pre-existence outside it.

This is the heart of Jennings' achievement *as a director* because there is nothing really spontaneous about these lit, rehearsed and repeatedly shot takes. These are not, as Vaughan noted, Direct Cinema, much less the result of the happenstance of voyeurism. Jennings' accomplishment in this regard can be measured by the contrast it makes with the performances routinely obtained and accepted by his fellow documentary directors.

However the 'strangely memorable quality' of these shots across the oeuvre as a whole should not be credited to Jennings alone. All his key films apart from *A Diary for Timothy* were edited by Stewart McAllister, about whom Vaughan has written a splendid biography significantly entitled *Portrait of an Invisible Man*. Vaughan, with much justice, attributes the 'hairsbreadth' judgments that make up the memorable shots to McAllister; or rather to a two-headed beast best thought of as Jennings/McAllister (or 'Jennings').

Apart from acute observation, almost all the films are also marked by an extraordinary formal density, which again can be attributed as much to Jennings/McAllister as to Jennings alone. The juxtapositioning of individual shots (which often have little or no spatial or temporal connection with each other); the relationship of those shots to the soundtrack (multi-layered, overlaid, often without direct connection to image); and the resultant complexity of overall structure, are without precedent – or indeed much emulation, despite the high regard in which many documentarists hold Jennings.

Of course, film-makers had long since realised that juxtapositions created new levels of meaning, the sum of two shots having more force than that of either shot individually. Enhancing this in Jennings' case was his obsession with the ambiguities of language, especially poetic language, which was at the heart of his scholarly concerns during his time at Cambridge in the 20s. (One of his friends there was William Empson whose *Seven Types of Ambiguity* was to be a major mid-century work of literary criticism.) Ambiguities and resonances on the page become multiple levels of connectivity on the screen. What is pioneering about the Jennings/McAllister approach is the achievement of syntheses, not synthesis.

The films are replete with Baroque moments where two soundtracks, one perhaps continuing from a previous shot, carry over new shots. The whole is connected by subtle notions of contrast and analogy often informed by an abstract framework of implicit reference to British, usually English, social mores, traditions, history and literature. Such moments constitute nothing less than the filmic equivalent of ambiguity run riot, the seventeenth-century poetic 'conceit': 'A fanciful, ingenious or witty notion; and affectation of thought or style.' That is what is new about them.

And, it must be admitted, they are not to everybody's taste. Conceits, especially on film, also run the danger of being too clever by half. The medium is, self-evidently, far from ideal for dealing with abstraction of any kind. Thinking up impeccable logical justifications for constructing sequences, especially montage sequences, where there is no immediate demand to maintain spatial or temporal continuity, is a commonplace of the documentary editing process. The only trouble is that such justifications are indiscernible by the audience. After all, they have not been living with the shots for months. For them the subtle structure is whizzing past at twenty-four frames a second (or its various video equivalents). The result, as Dai Vaughan once characterised it, is more often than not a film which 'works better in the head than on the screen'. The unique war-time achievement of Jennings and McAllister (and McAllister's assistants who adopted his style) was that this pitfall was almost always avoided.

The hovering presence of McAllister, the invisible man, means that the formal innovations of the films are somewhat less celebrated by settled opinion than is the quality of acute observation which can be more cleanly assigned to Jennings himself. (Although, here too the auteurists need to note the contribution of cameramen – which they all were despite the fact that the Union actually allowed some women into that grade during the War – and the use of stock shots, that endless pillaging of the archive which is a largely un-remarked characteristic of much classic documentary.) So less is made of this flamboyant editing style by Jennings enthusiasts perhaps exactly because it offends against a simple auteurist vision of film-making.[5] Knowledge of McAllister's contribution to the final product clouds such a vision. And on some films McAllister's interventions went beyond the cutting-room. Jennings' sound recordist, Ken Cameron:

> there's no doubt that Mac made a tremendous contribution to that film [*Listen to Britain*]. He told Humphrey what he needed – 'Humphrey, go out and shoot this' – and Humphrey did it. A tremendous influence on the film.

Responsibility becomes collective. The formal attractiveness of the films, their high intelligence and dizzy displays of technical virtuosity, is a major source of pleasure and a second clearly distinguishing mark of the work of 'Jennings'.

I also have to acknowledge, however, in the particular context of this book, that *Fires Were Started*, as the most overtly dramatic and conventional of this group of films, actually contains fewer 'conceits' of this kind than do the others. This is in no way to downgrade McAllister's contribution to the film or to suggest it totally lacks the complexities of contrast and juxtaposition that mark the rest of the oeuvre. It is only to acknowledge that these occasions are less exuberant, less central than they are, say, in *A Diary for Timothy*. But they are still there and the poetic technique, even in *Fires Were Started*, is as Anderson described it:

The films succeed as poetry through the style which Jennings fashioned as a unique instrument for the expression of his vision. Simple images composed with enormous care, rarely rhetorical with almost no movement of the camera; natural sound selectively used; music and dialogue expressive of mood and character not of fact. In the subtlest most intuitive way, image is juxtaposed with image, sound overlapping, binding and contrasting one time and place and emotion with another. The world created is moral, humane, peculiarly innocent. Its magic can be analysed only up to a certain point, then it must simply be experienced.

5

....

'FILMS OF BRITAIN AT WAR'

Acute observation is uncontroversially seen as an advantage in a documentarist. Formal complexity, although rejectable on populist (or, better, quasi-populist) grounds, is normally considered to be at least a source of interest. But what I think must be admitted as the third component of Jennings' greatness is by no means regarded as a 'good thing' by the *bien-pensants*. As a result, settled opinion downplays or even ignores Jennings the propaganda master.

For scholars, such as Jacques Elul, propaganda is multi-faceted and has a complex relationship to truth. It is not necessarily limited to active hectoring, which Elul calls 'direct propaganda'. It can also be 'sociological' (or 'indirect'), more concerned with structuring underlying attitudes or behaviour patterns than with provoking direct action. In Elul's view, most propaganda is indirect, seeking 'no longer to transform an opinion, but to arouse an active and mythical belief'. Covert or overt, this is now its main function:

> The spectator will be much more disposed to believe in the grandeur of France when he has seen a dozen films on French petroleum, railroads, or jetliners. The ground must be sociologically prepared before one can proceed to direct prompting. Sociological propaganda can be compared to ploughing, direct propaganda to sowing.

Ploughing was Jennings' approach. He was a champion ploughman and in my view, *Fires Were Started*, not (say) *Triumph des Willens*, is the real propaganda masterwork of the BFI list.

This is not, however, to claim that Jennings' films were massively effective in maintaining belief in the greatness of Britain at war, or even in sustaining national morale. We don't know what effect they had because evidence is almost impossible to come by. Given how we endlessly row about the contemporary effects of violent images, for example, it is inevitable that we are never going to agree about the extent to which the war-time propaganda effort was successful at achieving any given specific X or Y.

During the war, anthropologist Tom Harrisson sustained Mass Observation to map British attitudes, using various techniques including questionnaires. Ever after Harrisson was dismissive of the propaganda effect of all these films on the domestic war-time audience. Firstly (and he is not alone in claiming this) people went to the cinema to escape the War. But cinema newsreels ensured that there was no escape:[6] 'The newsreel, on our evidence, gravely over-played the war emphasis. People just got fed up with that.' But, more than that, Harrisson remained sceptical about the effects of film in general:

> Morale is not, in my view – and I spent years studying it in those days – affected by things like film. Pints of beer affect morale; being healthy and all kinds of things affect morale. But official films never really came into it in people's own estimate of what affected them in the crunch.

But what is an 'effect' in this context? Harrisson himself was vague about this. In the same interview he said: 'We found that films about the sea and the Navy always got a very good reaction.' Jennings' films could get a 'good reaction' too. Roger Manvell spent the war organising non-theatrical screenings of official films – around a hundred shows a week. He would always include the Jennings titles as they became available because of:

> the poetic and emotional lift they gave to the programme as a whole. I do not exaggerate when I say that members of the audiences under emotional stress of war, especially during

the earlier, more immediate alarming years, frequently wept as a result of Jennings' appeal to the rich cultural heritage of Britain.

Yet Harrisson claimed that they had no 'effect' on morale, or no 'lasting' effect.

Anyway, there was another, overseas, dimension to the propaganda effort, especially over the representation of the Blitz and the Battle of Britain. In Nicholas Pronay's view, 'a great deal came to depend on what the world thought about Britain's ability to resist the onslaught'. This was a very difficult propaganda task, as was well understood at the time. In October 1940 during the early days of the Blitz, Foreign Office official A. W. G. Randall wrote:

> The policy of emphasising the horrors of the bombardment of London in order to excite admiration for the people who are standing up to those horrors, is likely, in some foreign countries, to have the effect of exciting admiration for the efficient way in which Germany is laying London in ruins.

Fires Were Started deals with this problem firstly by turning it into history. The film was made well after the British and the rest of the world knew that the Blitz had failed or, to be even more positive, that the 'Battle of Britain' had been won. Set in 1940–41, the film was shot a year later and released in 1943. The date of the setting is established in an opening title:

> When the Blitz first came to
> Britain, its fires were fought
> by brigades of regular and auxiliary
> firemen, each independent of the
> rest though linked by
> reinforcement.
>
> In the stress of battle, lessons
> were learned which led in August,
> 1941 to the formation of a
> unified National Fire Service.

> This is a picture of the earlier
> days – the bitter days of winter
> and spring 1940/41 – played by the
> firemen and women themselves.

Moreover, Jennings' decision to make a film of the immediate past was perhaps fortuitous because there was no continuous Blitz during the autumn and winter of 1941–42 when he was researching the project and preparing his treatments; and there was no full Blitz when he was filming in the spring and early summer of 1942. The National Fire Service, which had come into being only weeks before Jennings began work on the project, could not yet be observed, much less filmed, in fully stretched action.

The perceived propaganda difficulty demanded that the enemy be ignored as much as possible. No planes are identified. No distant dog-fights figure. The fires are started without human agency. As the title-card has it, the Blitz 'came to Britain' as a sort of meteorological phenomenon, an act of God. The BBC news bulletin phrase which gives the film its title 'fires were started' also reflects the same policy of not alluding to the Germans. 'They'll be raiding tonight' is the closest *Fires Were Started* comes to mentioning the enemy.

The film also copes with this problem more specifically by demonstrating that, although the warehouse is gutted and Jacko, described in one of Jennings' treatments as 'a Cockney saint', dies, the crucial arms ship is untouched. As with Dunkirk, mere survival becomes decisive victory. In the dawn after the raid Johnny is asked whether it has

'Don't do nothing silly, will you?': Jacko is warned by his 'wife'

been a bad night: 'Bad night? You wanna go down the road and look over the wall. There's a boat down there, good as new. She ain't got a scratch on 'er – it's a sight for sore eyes.' In other words, the raid fails. This failure is reinforced at the film's close as the arms ship moves (screen right) along the Thames while Jacko's coffin is carried through the churchyard to rest (screen left). Stoic resistance is transformed into triumph – indirect, sociological propaganda for the Home Front and allies and neutrals. The spectator is presented with an image of British greatness unbowed by ferocious attack. This message is made all the more powerful by virtue of the fact that when the film was released, Britain had survived that phase of the Blitz.

That we cannot demonstrate how effective or otherwise *Fires Were Started* and the other films were, does not reduce Jennings' status as a propagandist. We have never allowed a test of utility to condition our evaluation of the documentary genre. For instance, the British Documentary Film Movement made many films about perennial social problems in the 1930s; but the fact that the problems are still with us and the films can be said, crudely, to have had no effect, is not factored into our evaluation of them. *Triumph des Willens*, likewise, is deemed to be the ultimate propaganda film but there is no evidence that anybody ever embraced Nazism as a result of seeing it. On the contrary, the film lives as an awful warning, an endlessly plundered source of *anti*-Nazi imagery. Nobody has ever used *Fires Were Started* or the rest of Jennings' work against the grain in that way. And, *pace* Harrisson, the degree to which, despite some revisionism, the image of Britain's Home Front war (enshrined most memorably on the screen in films such as *Fires Were Started*) remains intact is surely a measure of the effectiveness of these works as sociological propaganda.

The secret of the Jennings oeuvre's success seems to be his endless ability to substitute for direct propaganda (which almost always involves a big lie of one sort or another) various small economies with the truth which constitute a central technique of the sociological style. These are sugar-coated by being placed in the context of, or juxtaposed with, a reality which meshed with contemporary audience experience. This reality is often expressed quite negatively and would have been avoided at all costs by lesser propagandists (such as Leni Riefenstahl). It is the strength of the Jennings approach that such negatives are incorporated into the message and become the basis upon which the actual sociological

'We musn't work too hard, my friends.' B.A., Joe, Rumbold and the Heavy Unit

propaganda can rest. As Elul puts it: 'Propaganda must respect local facts, otherwise it would destroy itself. ... Existing opinion is not to be contradicted, but utilised.'

The best example of this is in the opening expository sequence of *Fires Were Started*. The men have just come on watch at 14Y and they are engaged in routine chores – washing steps, peeling potatoes, re-equipping the Heavy Unit (H.U.) appliance which has just been returned from the maintenance garage. The sense of bustle is increased by cross-cutting these activities with the arrival of Barrett. In the midst of this, B.A., who is working on the H.U., waves his hands to his two colleagues in a negative gesture which he will use again in the film: 'We mustn't work too hard, my friends. This job must last till one!' B.A. is later revealed as a source of cheap trouser-braces. The coded reference to black-market activity and his comic laziness do not, of course, detract one iota from B.A.'s efficiency as an auxiliary fireman; but his ironic view of the task in hand does constitute a sort of leavening of the film's heroics.

Such minor negative authenticities are the key to the film's effectiveness as a persuasive communication. In *Fires Were Started* this trope becomes something more than just, in a phrase of Dilys Powell, 'ironic in the English manner'. It also embraces human frailty. One of the W.A.F.S. telephone operators in 14 Local Control, for example, covers her face in a gesture of tiredness; Barrett mistakes a sewer cover for a water hydrant ('That ain't a bleedin' hydrant, it's a sewer!'); hoses are pointed in the wrong direction ('No, not up there, put it down!'); people go missing ('Where the hell are you?'); the crew hit the deck as a bomb goes off ('What a lot of windy bastards we are!') – all these examples

Barrett mistakes a sewer cover

'No, not up there': Dykes, Jacko and Rumbold on the roof

'What a lot of windy bastards we are!'

undercut the main propaganda message of indomitable spirit expressed through casual courage. The entire structure of heroic stoicism which pervades the film is, it seems to me, grounded in these all too human, unheroic moments.

What is happening here is that such concessions, if you will, to the shared reality of the audience, who knew very well the levels of disenchantment in play during the Blitz, allow the film to do its propaganda job. When the chips are down, when the bombs fall and the fires blaze and firemen are injured or die, there is no question of dereliction of duty, no sense that anybody will not come up to scratch.

Take the injured W.A.F.S. operator in 14 Control, for example, who apologises for being interrupted by a bomb blast. No mention of the bomb. The stiff upper-lip personified. Yet so well laid are the foundations of authenticity (as it were) in the instances I have just cited, that Jennings' use of this clichéd image and the obvious fakery of the firewoman's wound do not detract from the propaganda power of the moment.

I do not claim that this deprecatory approach is innovative. On the contrary it is the essence of a particular style of English propaganda traceable back to Shakespeare. In *Henry V*, for example, the king visits the common soldiers before the Battle of Agincourt bringing 'a little touch of Harry in the night'. One of them, the Cockney Bates, is B.A.'s direct ancestor. When the disguised king suggests that Henry himself may be frightened by the superiority of the French force and may be just putting on a show of bravery, Bates replies:

He may show what outward courage he will; but I believe, as cold a night as 'tis, he could wish himself in Thames up to the neck; – and so I would he were, and I by him, at all adventures, so we were quit here.
King: By my troth, I will speak my conscience of the King. I think he would not wish himself anywhere but where he is.
Bates: Then I would he were here alone; so should he be sure to be ransomed, and many poor men's lives saved.

This is a most curious sentiment to find in the greatest patriotic text in English literature; but, equally, it is a clue to that greatness. Without Bates' human desire to be somewhere – anywhere – else, would 'We few, we happy few, we band of brothers' a few scenes later work anything like as well? The propaganda message is made stronger by the injection of a measure of authentic nay-saying.

This ability to round out the reality of the people filmed counterbalances Jennings' use of stereotypes. The documentary tradition in which he was working depended very much on stereotyping, if only because the legitimacy of the films' claim on the real often required that particular moments, actions, events or people stand as instances of the general. In the tradition's founding film, *Nanook of the North*, it is one Inuit, Allarkariallak, playing 'Nanook' the stereotyped great hunter, who represents all such hunters and, indeed, all Inuit; but 'Nanook' also has a very distinct personality – which we have to assume, since Allarkariallak was not a trained actor, actually was his own. For the British Documentary Movement, the use of the particular to represent the general led to a tendency to cast subjects rather as the Soviet theory of film typage required. Individuals were instantly recognisable as general stereotypical social types – Cockney 'saints' or unflappable W.A.F.S., for instance.

The Cockney was particularly useful in propaganda terms, since that image had been vying for nearly a century with stereotypes of country people, peasant, yeoman or squire, to embody the soul of the nation. According to Gareth Stedman Jones, in the late 1800s Cockneys had been transformed by the charitable work of the Pearly Kings and Queens and the songs of music-hall stars like Albert (*'Knocked 'em in the Old Kent Road'*) Chevalier from their original stereotype as low-life gamblers and petty criminals, into what T. S. Eliot called 'that part of the English nation which has perhaps the greatest vitality'. Kipling made Tommy Atkins the backbone of the imperial army before 1914. After the First World War, the Tories tried in their rhetoric to replace Cockneys with rural folk; but the Christmas 1937 smash-hit *Me and My Girl* and the *Lambeth Walk* craze that followed, restored the London proletariat to its earlier pre-eminence. It is no propaganda accident that *Fires Were Started* is set in the East End and that Cockneys dominate the cast.

Jennings' strength is that, like 'Nanook', his loveable Cockney firemen and his stiff-upper-lipped firewomen also have their own distinct personalities. The stereotypes are the heroes on whom the propaganda message depends. The individuals are the all-too-human beings whose unheroic blemishes disguise the propaganda.

6

. . . .

'THIS IS WHAT WE WERE LIKE – THE BEST OF US'

Beyond incorporating these ironic negatives and debilities to ensure that the audience was comfortable with, or indeed would not consciously perceive, the propaganda message, there is another distinction between the hectoring, direct propaganda approach and Jennings' style. This too relies on a grounding in reality, but distorts or mythologises largely through sins of omission. As Lindsay Anderson suggested in the phrase I have used as the title for this chapter: 'This is what we were like – the best of us.' The less than best, never mind the worst, get short shrift. Thus, much is omitted.

The conventions of the time, for instance, simply did not permit authentic language – this proved to be a problem for the Documentary Movement from the introduction of sound on and, during the War, it limited the dialogue of service-based feature films as well. Even the word 'bloody' was more or less forbidden. *Fires Were Started* contains only one instance: 'Get down off that bloody roof!!!!' There's also 'Hell', 'bastards', 'bleedin'', 'Gor' blimey'. To the original audience this must have sounded daringly authentic – 'maybe for the first time – proper working class dialogue' – although it was still a rather feeble reflection of reality.

A more significant omission is the fact that civil order was a good deal more stretched than is suggested in Jennings' or, indeed, in the rest of British war-time film production. In truth, in a few blitzed cities

'Get down off that bloody roof!!!!'

outside London the social fabric did come close to tearing. Black-marketeering, for example, was endemic; and there were 60,000 conscientious objectors. And so on.

As for the fire service itself, Jennings finds no space for the everyday blimpish stupidities of the organisation – apart from the scene in which Jacko is reminded that he had got into trouble for painting his axe handle black, a colour reserved for superior officers. In fact from the outset of the Blitz there is evidence of a fair degree of near-disastrous farce, as documented in the official HMSO history of the London Brigade, by Sally Holloway. The first German attack was on major oil installations at the mouth of the Thames, outside the L.F.B.'s ground:

> The fire was not contained, nor was the temper of the London officer improved when, an hour later, the local officer in charge said he was going home now because he was only a volunteer ... a fiery Principal Officer from the L.F.B. immediately ordered fifty pumps and three fireboats to the scene, but was told this was not possible as they were outside the London area and only the local officer in charge – a Cambridge 'don' – could make such a decision. Nor could he be disturbed. The hour was late and he would be in bed and asleep.

The jealously guarded autonomy of the local brigades and widespread arrogance, pomposity and stupidity meant that the entire response was nearly calamitous. In the aftermath of the Coventry raid of 14-15 November 1940, for example, city officials were still declining to provide emergency water reservoirs until the question was settled concerning who was to bear the cost. In Liverpool in May 1941, the Chief Fire Officer refused to inspect the situation on the ground because a Home Office memorandum said C.F.O.s were not to leave their control centres. The moves to establish a National Fire Service, referred to in the opening title of *Fires Were Started*, were, therefore, fraught. After the decision was finally taken, there was a last deranged, blimpish problem about the insignia of the new service. Military pips or stars were objected to even as the Bill to create the N.F.S. was being placed before Parliament. Only after pump impellers were suggested as an alternative did the Bill become law on 22 May 1941, twelve days after the final major raid of this phase of the Blitz. The N.F.S. was operational by September of that year. In *Fires*

Were Started the pre-N.F.S. system is shown as stretched, but working perfectly.

Jennings also ignores the tensions which existed between the regular firemen of the L.F.B. and the A.F.S. volunteers. Most of the hostility arose from differentials between the A.F.S. and regular fire brigade pay scales. The A.F.S. paid significantly lower wages. Nor is there any hint in the film that, at least until the Blitz began, volunteering for the A.F.S. was somewhat suspect, a way of avoiding the call-up into the military.

The film does not accurately reflect the important role women played in the fire service, either. The range of their duties extended well beyond the operation of switchboards and canteens (which is all that Jennings shows us). For example, Holloway quotes Betty Cuthbert, the eleventh woman to volunteer and who eventually became the W.A.F.S. Chief Officer: 'I was trained as a fireman – in everything – and I was given a trailer pump to put on the back of my Wolseley car so that I would be available for any emergency.' One woman, Gillian Tanner, won a George Medal for delivering petrol to appliances during a bombing attack.

The women were also the source of much anxiety, as servicemen worried that their wives and girlfriends who joined the W.A.F.S. were in far too close proximity to the firemen. Although Jennings cast a number of conventionally attractive young firewomen to play in the film ('Pretty, trousers' is one description), none of this tension is highlighted either. Just before the raid, B.A. twirls Mrs Townsend briefly around the Rec. A slightly dishevelled young woman in the mobile canteen during the dawn sequence warrants a 'Bless you, my beautiful!' as she hands out a cup of tea. There is one other Jennings/McAllister moment when the Heavy Unit is being delivered to Y at the beginning of the film. The mechanic/driver is in the watch room. In a synch close-up, he remarks of the appliance, 'She looks all right', but the film cuts, ambiguously, to W.A.F.S. Eileen White. Otherwise, the crew and the women never flirt.

The logic of Jennings' language in the opening intertitle, that 'lessons were learned', promises a film which will reveal at least some of these problems and attitudes. It does no such thing. But it is not that Jennings was unaware of them. In the various research notes, synopses and outlines, treatments and almost full-scale scripts that he produced for

'Bless you, my beautiful!'

B.A., Barrett, Johnny and the
black market braces

the film between October 1941 and January 1942, there are references to all of the tensions and stresses, but none of those survived the production process. For example, in Jennings' treatment, dated '27 January 1942' ('The Fifth Treatment'), the conversation about the axes was to contain a reference to the ineffectiveness of the colour-coded system during night fires, but this is not in the film. (The treatment goes on to refer directly to the black market, as B.A. tries to sell his braces: 'The whole pair for half a dollar and no coupons or questions asked.' If filmed, this dialogue also was never edited in.)

A document called 'Bare Outlines of N.F.S. Story', written by Jennings in mid-December 1941, suggested that the film could 'perhaps' open with '*1. The man & his pal*'; that is, an L.F.B man and an A.F.S. man. In the 'Fifth Treatment'/script six weeks later this theme becomes a more realistic 'endless argument about rates of pay, compensation etc.' in the 14Y Rec. Room. In the final film, the stresses between the two services are reduced to an opaque comic remark over a game of snooker. Rumbold, one of the A.F.S. men, quips to the regular L.F.B. fireman, S/O Dykes: 'You fellows get three pairs of trousers and we only get one. You have to do so much sitting around.'

In this same treatment/script, Dykes was to reveal during a synch street conversation with a sailor that he had served in the Merchant Navy during the First World War: 'We was in the drink for 16 hours before we was picked up and I remember Pincher Martin, he says to me he says, "When we gets out of this, I'm going to join the Fire Brigade."' Not a skiver by any means, but in the final film the sailor becomes a civilian acquaintance and the synch we hear does not address the point: '…."when I get out of this," he says, "I'll join the Fire Brigade." "Did he?" "That's the funny part of it…"'.

Such a pattern of omission also informs the antiseptic relationships between the men and women; but in an early synopsis, dated '25.10.41', Jennings did have the women factory workers joshing with the firemen, 'having a bit of back-chat with just a wee hint of danger in it … it is going to be essential to get a good kind of invisible link between the firemen and the girls'. They, not the munitions ship, were to be in danger during the fire, but all this disappeared. Moreover, nowhere is there any suggestion that Jennings was thinking of showing the full range of W.A.F.S. activities. That women were so exposed to danger during the very period of *Fires Were Started* seems to have been considered to be bad for morale and unsuitable for the official MoI propaganda purposes of the film.

None of the synch dialogue of the 'Fifth Treatment'/script on these points made the final cut, although most of them did get on to the screen in another, fictional, film about the A.F.S. – *The Bells Go Down*, an Ealing production directed by Basil Dearden, also made in 1942. For example, in *The Bells Go Down* there is a comic black-market sub-plot about stolen barrels of Guinness, and the tension between the two services is also mentioned more than once: 'There's too much victimisation of the A.F.S.' As is pay: 'Money ain't so good, of course – but I like the job'; 'We're doing the same work as L.F.B. men, aren't we? We want the same rights. And we want the same pay.' And the notion that the A.F.S. men are avoiding duty: 'We ain't doing nothing, really,' says one ironically to a couple of uniformed soldiers. Finally, although the firewomen are still marginal, there is much romantic interest. Apparently, these themes, although acceptable within the propaganda framework of a commercial feature, were judged by the MoI and its Crown Film Unit to be too vexed to justify their inclusion in *Fires Were Started*.

To acknowledge that these omissions were (and are) big (or big-ish) lies, though, cannot be allowed to sanction a wholesale rewrite of the historical record. That there was a good deal less cohesion to the 'war spirit' than the myth suggests – more shirking, more black-marketeering, more rage and more fear – nevertheless cannot disguise the fact that there was no significant widespread breakdown of civil order, although that had been expected. And 60,000 conscientious objectors is a minuscule percentage of a population of 45 million plus. Nor did the fire service collapse. And there were many middle-class volunteers, so the fancy accents of the W.A.F.S. (which seem to get fancier the higher the level of control room they are working in), and the characters of Barrett (William Sansom) and Walters in the film are not inauthentic. Sansom, for example, was in fact in the A.F.S. long before Jennings began casting *Fires Were Started*.

Peter Stead summed up the situation in this way:

> The reputation of British cinema during the Second World War was to rest on a small number of films which, without endangering morale in any way, nevertheless depicted the war and the involvement of ordinary citizens in it in what was taken to be an honest way. With hindsight we can see that many aspects of the war were neglected and there was never any real attempt to communicate the *whole* truth. But there was sufficient integrity and vitality to convince contemporary audiences and critics...

I agree that Jennings was far from telling the *whole* truth; what makes him a propaganda master is that his partial truth, even after all these omissions, is still extremely compelling. Jennings put multifaceted characters on the screen who exhibited a realistic mixture of courage and human frailty. Equally importantly, he also placed them in a rich, essentially historical, social context. The effect of endowing these contemporary individual characters with a resonating collective past is the last element of his propaganda technique that I want to consider.

7

....

'THE PAST WITH THE PRESENT'

The presence of the past is crucial to all Jennings' films.

No element of wartime propaganda was more important than this notion of 'one nation'. It was the pivotal myth which lay at the heart of much war-time film-making. It conditioned casting and narrative to ensure that officers and men, the bourgeois and the proletarian, as well as the proverbial Englishman, Welshman and Scotsman (and occasional Irishman) appeared again and again in harmonious accord. This multi-national identity is moderately submerged in *Fires Were Started* because the Scotsman, Rumbold, and the Liverpool-Irishman, B.A., do not have pronounced accents; but the theme is still residually there.

The version of ethnicity that is presented is, however, very curious. What saved Jennings, and indeed others such as the Ealing film-makers, from a fascistic Little Englander dream of race is that this 'one nation' was built out of shared experience, history and place rather than a mythology of blood and soil. 'One nation' becomes scarcely an 'ethnic' concept at all. Thus the 'Fifth Treatment'/script can suggest that a Jewish fireman (to be named 'Solomon Isaacs') might be on a crew. This is not included in the final film, but a shot of a crew list blackboard prominently reveals that a 'Cohen' is on 14Y's strength. Barrett is seen asking his way to 14Y in a dockers' café, and is 'kindly and charmingly' given instructions in 'pidgin English' by its Chinese proprietor. This last does survive in the film as a brief street encounter

Barrett's encounter with a Chinese man. 'One nation' in action

with a Chinese man. This man, and Cohen, belong to the East End as much as any Cockney.

The image of a class society without friction, truly at ease with itself, is even more important than ethnicity to the 'one nation' theme in *Fires Were Started*. Most of the W.A.F.S. in the film, Barrett, Rumbold and Walters, are middle class but there is no strain between them and the Cockneys, even Cockneys in command such as Dykes. This harmony was absolutely central to Jennings, and it was grounded for him in the glories of a magnificent shared history and culture. Although there is much progressive opinion reflected in Jennings' other films, especially *A Diary for Timothy*, his veritable obsession with the past is the source of what school friend Marius Goring called Jennings' 'astonishing' conservatism.

In *Fires Were Started* Jennings' deep sense of cultural continuity is expressed through popular songs – the music-hall numbers, folk songs, contemporary hits which the men are constantly singing – and by two texts drawn from Raleigh and Shakespeare which Rumbold reads. Sir Walter Raleigh's address to Death is heard as the men are about to leave to fight the fire: 'O eloquent, just and mighty Death! whom none could advise, thou hast persuaded; what none hath dared, thou hast done...' This cues more realistic irony in Sub-Officer Dyke's response, which undercuts the moment in a friendly if stereotypically anti-intellectual Cockney way: 'Right ho, Colonel, we'll set that to music when we come back.'

As with the cleverness of the editing style, some find this use of Elizabethan speech hard to take – as did several critics at the time. *Documentary News Letter*, despite praising the film lavishly, was nevertheless damning about this exchange in which Jennings 'goes all arty for a moment'. But this was to miss how necessary these words are. In a realist film, how can English inarticulateness convey the heightened situation of the calm before the raid? Using the most cerebral of the crew (and a Scotsman) to read Raleigh solves the problem at least as well as having the men express their fears, or indeed anything deep, in their own words. That would, perhaps, have been even more unlikely than showing one of them reading aloud. And the use of the Raleigh address gives Jennings further crucial bonuses.

In propaganda terms, Raleigh's words are about the persistent inevitability of death ('so don't rage against it', is the message); but they also, by their antique nature, call up the ghosts of the very culture and polity which these men are about to defend with their lives. Jennings, more than any of his fellows, heard the constant echoes of an unbroken English past in the present. *Words for Battle*, made in 1941, is the clearest example of this, an eight-minute-long ambitious, if not entirely successful, attempt to escape from the norms of narrative by using a selection of classic literary texts as commentary over images of the Home Front. Hence *Documentary News Letter* condemns the classic quotations in *Fires Were Started* for being in Jennings' 'worst *Words for Battle* manner'; but they cannot be so attacked. Rather they are a reflection of Jennings' quite central and consistent vision of the historical 'skull beneath the skin' in contemporary life. According to Stuart Legg, he referred to this theme in his work as 'tying knots in history'.

In *The Poet and the Public*, a series of radio talks that Jennings broadcast in 1938, he was already quite clear about why this was important:

> That idea of extracting an idea of 'what I am' from the past is a thing that the poet does for himself and especially it is a thing that he can do for the community. I mean he can try and tell them who they are. Now he can't tell them who they are unless he does two things: unless he talks about the things that the community knows about, the things that they're interested in, and unless he also looks on the community's past – at the figures, the monuments, the achievements, the defeats or whatever it may be, that have made the community what it is.

Kevin Jackson suggests that Jennings the film-maker was just such an artist, a sort of celluloid Poet Laureate, working to 'remind a people of what they have been in the past and thereby suggest to them something of what they are in the present'.

Elsewhere Jennings contrasted this poetic use of the past with the work historians do. He saw their analytic toil as the disentangling of history 'shred by shred like plucking the strand out of a rope'. The poet, by contrast, 'might be compared to a man who cuts a short section of the whole rope. The only thing is he must cut it where it will not fall to pieces.' That he himself was adept at this is attested to in Manvell's recollection of how the use of the 'rich cultural heritage of Britain' in the films provoked extreme emotional responses in the war-time audience:

People found themselves being brought suddenly and movingly in touch with what was at stake if indeed the Nazi forces ... invaded and took over the conduct of their lives. ... Jennings made [audiences] aware of ... what exactly a successful invasion by Germany could mean in a country that had not been invaded for close to a thousand years. Few of the hundreds of wartime films made between 1940 and 1944 achieved this.

Although few had such developed theories about it, Jennings was not alone in feeling the weight of the past in this way. In July 1941 Noël Coward, for example, had responded to the Blitz in similar, albeit more populist, terms in his hit song *London Pride*:

> In our city darkened now, street and square and crescent,
> We can feel our living past in our shadowed present,
> Ghosts beside our starlit Thames
> Who lived and loved and died
> Keep throughout the ages London Pride

That same year, Jennings began the *I See London* poem: 'I see London. I see the dome of St Paul's like the forehead of Darwin...' Later in 1941 he wrote: 'Slowly – how slowly – but clearly enough England & Scotland & Wales are beginning to look at *life*: the way they did in 1400.'

'I see London': a Thames barge in full sail

The past is thus the bedrock upon which the myth of 'one nation' without class friction, so central to the propaganda of the films, rests. For Jennings it was history – conventional history, literary history, cultural history, even scientific and technological history – that bound the oppositional elements of the heroic and the unheroic – and, indeed, nation and classes – together. This is why the *Documentary News Letter*'s view that Dykes' response to Rumbold reflected Jennings' 'embarrassment' at his own 'artiness' was so mistaken. Rather it is Jennings having his cake and eating it (as usual) – the archaic language speaks to the propaganda message in play, while the ironic Cockney response reflects a realism that disguises the propaganda.

Rumbold's second reading in the film's penultimate sequence functions in the same way. This time Shakespeare is used to deliver an oblique eulogy to the dead Jacko, which again could not be performed realistically or with any ease by the men in the film:

> Ay, in the catalogue ye go for men;
> As hounds and greyhounds, mongrels, spaniels, curs,
> Shoughs, water-rugs, and demi-wolves are clept
> All by the name of dogs...

The speech conveys a subtle sense of class and sacrifice, but it is cross-cut prosaically with the image of Mrs Townsend pouring the exhausted men cups of tea. It is hard to see how the crew, including Barrett, could articulate so elaborate a lament for a lost comrade, the 'dog' Jacko, in their own words. (As I have pointed out, 'Jacko's copped it, I tell you. ... Copped it!' is the best that B.A. can do at the scene of the tragedy.) And again, Shakespeare, a writer recently reconfirmed as the embodiment of a millennium of English achievement, carries like Raleigh all the resonances of the culture under threat by the Blitz. When Rumbold finishes, B.A. can say, 'Come on, chums, snap out of it!' and the film can proceed to its coda, the triumphal departure of the arms ship and Jacko's burial.

The subtle methods of Jennings the propagandist always remind me of a judgment given in the House of Lords in 1942. The case concerned those war-time regulations which gave the Home Secretary powers – positively dictatorial powers – to detain enemy aliens and anybody else, including British subjects, suspected of hostile 'origin or associations'. Could these regulations be subject to review in the courts, or were they a matter for executive discretion only, a discretion that could not be questioned? Lord Atkin delivered the following ringing judgment declaring that such decisions had to be subject to legal oversight:

> It has always been one of the pillars of freedom, one of the principles of liberty for which on recent authority we are now fighting, that the judges are no respecters of persons and stand between the subject and any attempted encroachments on his liberty by the executive, alert to see that any coercive action is justified in law. In this case I have listened to argument which might have been addressed acceptably to the Court of the King's Bench in the time of Charles I.

This passage enshrines for me the authentic voice of liberal England, unfazed by the deadly threats of the day. But behind it lies a more complex, paradoxical situation: Atkin was overruled – 4:1 (of course!). Jennings' strength is that he captures something – much – of this paradox. On the one hand there was without question a sense of community under fire and an affirmation of fundamental liberal values; just as, against that, the old régime persisted unaltered and used this feeling of unity to preserve its privileges and position. In the same paradoxical way, *Fires Were Started* celebrates an essentially working-class collective effort, giving voice and dignity to a group normally at this time denied both on the screen, while simultaneously re-affirming all the traditional (oppressive) continuities of British, or rather English, life.

An essentially working-class effort. 'Making up' in the dawn

8

. . . .

'JENNINGS' FILMS ARE ALL DOCUMENTARIES'

One last paradox remains.

Despite all its elements of authenticity, how can *Fires Were Started* be in any meaningful sense a *documentary*? For us today, after four decades of the observational 'fly-on-the-wall' style of Direct Cinema, all these preparations, re-workings, scriptings and endlessly repeated takes render the film moot as a 'documentary'. Of course, for Jennings and his contemporaries, this was simply not an issue. The use of non-actors, actual firemen, and the legitimations of various types of prior witness were enough to mark the project as a documentary, re-enactments notwithstanding.

Grierson's people had inherited a persistent tradition of re-enactment, including the use of specially constructed sets. The pioneering documentarist Robert Flaherty, for example, had Allarkariallak build an enlarged, half-sided igloo in *Nanook of the North*. Grierson himself had a mocked-up trawler cabin constructed on the dockside for his first film, *Drifters*. Synchronous sound made general re-enactment or reconstruction a routine necessity from the mid-30s on. The equipment would allow for nothing else. As Ricky Leacock noted of Flaherty's *Louisiana Story*, shot between 1946–48, four years after *Fires Were Started*:

> I saw that when we were using small cameras [to shoot silent footage], we had tremendous flexibility, we could do anything we wanted. ... The moment we had to shoot dialogue, lip-synch – everything had to be locked down. ... We had heavy disk recorders, and the camera that, instead of weighing six pounds, weighed 200 pounds, a sort of monster.

Filming re-enactments was central to the 'creative treatment of actuality', as Grierson's famous definition of the documentary has it.[7] It was not only permitted; it was in fact the cardinal mark of what made documentary different from other forms of non-fictional film-making, such as newsreels. As a 1948 definition, quoted by Richard Barsam, put it, documentary film embraced 'all methods of recording on celluloid any aspect of reality either by factual shooting or by sincere and justifiable reconstruction...'. Documentarists were driven, as it were, to reconstruction because of the initial failure of the documentary to develop modes of representing time and space on the screen which were specific to this particular film form. Instead, from *Nanook of the North* on, there was a tendency simply to utilise the grammar of representation which had been developed primarily by the fiction film in Hollywood. Flaherty understood the need to impose these conventions on his 'real life' material in order to construct a story. This led him, in the second half of *Nanook*, to discover a documentary form distinct from both the fiction film on the one hand and other forms of non-fiction (e.g. newsreel) on the other. As film theorist Bill Nichols has said: 'Documentary operates in the crease between life as lived and life as narrativised'; but making narratives required intervention not just through reconstruction, but at the most basic 'factual shooting' level as well.

In the single-camera studio world of the fiction film, actions were routinely repeated to achieve a variety of different shots so that audience interest could be sustained and action would be continuous across cuts. In the documentary world outside the studios, unless an action were itself repeated, this meant that non-actors were required to repeat themselves even if they would not have done so in the absence of the camera. In truth, 'factual shooting' as conceived of in 1948 – even 'silent' factual shooting – was only rarely as-it-happens 'fly-on-the-wall' filming. The significance of Hollywood's grammatical tyranny (as it might be called) for the documentary was therefore profound, as shooting almost inevitably involved some measure of direct intervention.

On this basis, it is easy to attack – as I and others have done – the factual pretensions of the classic documentary. Surely, no 'actuality' (that is, evidence and witness) can remain after all this brilliant interventionist 'creative treatment' (that is, artistic and dramatic structuring) has gone on? Grierson's enterprise was too self-contradictory to sustain any claim on the real, and renders the term 'documentary' meaningless. But perhaps this opinion overstates the case. John Corner has a very good point when he asks of us critics: 'Isn't it possible for audiences to believe in factors of degree and interplay here rather than to be caught between two absolutes?'

Not least because I have lived so closely with *Fires Were Started* for the better part of a year, I do now agree with Corner that there can be a middle ground. It is possible for significant reflections of 'actuality' to survive the 'creative treatment' of the film-making craft. Despite the elasticities of the witness process, despite the re-enactments, despite all the paraphernalia of fiction film production, a film like *Fires Were Started* is still as fine a factual record – a document – of 'what we were like' as any available. It has, in abundance, 'documentary value' (to use another famous phrase of Grierson's). And by contrasting it with the fictional *The Bells Go Down*, which I have already mentioned, it is possible to highlight exactly what this 'value' might be.

War-time documentary features such as *Fires Were Started* were very often matched by full-scale fictional feature films on the same topics. *The Way Ahead* has its counterpart in the documentary *Coastal Command*. The Ealing film *San Demetrio London* parallels *Western Approaches*. Often an opening title, as in *San Demetrio London*, stresses the factual basis of the incidents upon which the feature film was based.

In this series of parallels, the two films which are in closest lock-step with each other are *Fires Were Started* and *The Bells Go Down*, the latter starring Tommy Trinder in his second 'straight' film for Michael Balcon at Ealing. So akin are they that the same title was at one point being suggested for both of them.[8] The Ealing production, which was Basil Dearden's first solo directing credit, was written by Roger MacDougall[9] and starred James Mason as well as the comedian Trinder. It began principal photography in April, a little later than the 'National Fire Service story' Jennings was shooting.

Comparing the two suggests a case for documentary difference, despite the full-scale re-enactments of the Jennings' film. The basic structures of both the documentary and the fiction are virtually identical. Both are set in the London docks. A motley crew of firemen is introduced. Daily life in the station and training is shown. A major fire is tackled where the water gives out. In each film, central characters die in the attempt to bring a fire under control. Both films finish with a church service. The feature film was marketed as: 'A film of flaming heroism. ... A story of real people told with thrilling realism.' The *Daily Mail* called it: 'A picture of the people for the people.'

The plot of the fiction film starts before the War and runs through the 1940–41 autumn and winter Blitz. It offers a number of sub-plots – a couple postpone their marriage because of the outbreak of war; they then marry, and produce the child who is christened in the last sequence of the film. (Although seen buying second-hand furniture and living in a slum, 'Nan', the wife, played by Philippa Hiatt, has a very posh accent, thus illustrating the then cardinal rule of British cinema that anything other than cut-glass tones was incompatible with sexual allure.) Another character, played by Mervyn Johns, is stealing barrels of Guinness for the black-market from a ship in the dock and he joins the A.F.S. to escape the local 'bobby'. Tommy Trinder appears to steal James Mason's girl, 'Susie' (played by Meriel Forbes) – who, being no better than she should be, has a marginally less upper-crust accent than Nan but still doesn't sound like she's ever been to the East End, much less lived there. There are also a number of fires in the film, ranging from a comic blaze involving heavily stereotyped Italian café owners, to the climatic raid which starts a conflagration at the hospital where Nan is having her baby.

The first difference, then, is that *The Bells Go Down* has a much more complex narrative overall, which the documentary does not begin to match. *Fires Were Started*, despite its numerous fictional elements and techniques, including planted back-story plot points and the false 'death' and burial service of a fireman, nevertheless retains its documentary credibility in the first instance because of this narrative simplicity – a single day, a single fire.

Arising from this is a second distinction: Jennings' firemen exist only in the civil sphere. Their personal lives are reduced to one shot in Johnny's back-garden and two scenes showing Jacko's 'wife'. On the other hand, the central characters in *The Bells Go Down*, James Mason as the L.F.B. man and Trinder, who plays an A.F.S. volunteer, both have mates and parents in addition to romantic entanglements. Indeed, the L.F.B./A.F.S. conflict is personalised as a tension between Mason and Trinder over Forbes. The fish-and-chip shop kept by Trinder's mother and the pub run by James Mason's parents are major locations.

Moreover *Fires Were Started* adopts the traditional documentary tone; that is to say, it is (to use a phrase of Nichols') 'a discourse of sobriety'. In opposition to this, the fiction film goes in for comic relief, guaranteed by the presence of its star, Trinder, who was a major vaudevillian. So, in yet another sub-plot, Tommy acquires a comically unsuccessful greyhound. He is also given space for some vaudeville-style routines; for example, he toys with the vital telephone links in the Watch Room to place a bet on his dog. Trinder's antics contrast with the limited levities of 'B.A.' and the sing-songs of the documentary. The restriction of personal relationships to the civil sphere and the serious tone are other major elements in the 'documentary-ness' of *Fires Were Started*.

There is also a difference between the editing styles of the two films. Vaughan maintains that Jennings and McAllister were cutting to maximise the information about the service rather than for drama – even during the climatic fire.

> The pace of the fire-fighting sequence is neither that of drama nor that of vérité: it is the pace required for the clear explanation of a procedure: the pace, in a word, of the instructional documentary.

This leads to a further documentary element located in the film's general treatment of the very business of fire-fighting. Despite the feature film's title and its gestures towards a training sequence, in the documentary there is far more illustration of the fire service at work. The 'how-to-fight-a-fire' element, if you will, replaces the personal melodramas and comedy routines of the fiction. *Fires Were Started* spends time with explicit explanations of fire-fighting techniques and uses much specialised language. There are more references to detailed procedures such as the use of fire floats, emergency water supplies, the re-enforcement system, and trivial facts such as hatchet handles being painted different colours. Maps and establishing shots of various Watch and Control Rooms figure large, if not entirely effectively. (Without question, Jennings' painstaking efforts to explain the abandoned pre-N.F.S. structure of command, mainly through the crude use of explicit establishing shots of signs and maps, are the least successful part of the

14 District Control

Observation Post Control

Brigade Control – The Chief
Officer Commanding

film. This was not entirely his fault, since the various controls – local, district, O.P. and brigade – employ W.A.F.S. with telephones who answer every call at whatever level, confusingly, 'Control'. Even the national centre, which is not shown, is referred to as 'Home Office Fire Control'!)

These distinctions, then, impact on the most obvious set of contrasts – between firemen and actors; or between some studio sets but real external locations and a totally staged setting; or between a measure of authenticated dialogue and incident as against wholly invented melodrama and comedy.

If we dismiss *Fires Were Started* as a documentary, or begin to reclassify it as a form unknown to Jennings and his contemporaries such as 'drama-documentary', in effect we do so on the basis that we have considered only the crudest tests of authenticity alone to find it wanting.

The case for the prosecution here is that in *Fires Were Started* the 'real' people, the 'real' locations and the 'real' events are not as authentic as they seem. The real people have assumed names. They are not in their true locations. The interior locations are sets. The fire is fabricated. The death is faked. Actual people and places have been converted into the typical by the film-makers; and the people are not always guaranteed to be doing what they usually do, but what they did or, even, what others like them did.

This dismissal, though, ignores the cumulative force of the other more subtle elements of authenticity that I have been outlining: the simplicity and witnessed truthfulness of the plot and much of the dialogue, the narrow focus of the characters, the patina of details most vividly reinforced by the status of the actors as 'real' fire personnel and the reality of the non-studio locations.

Contrast the fires in the two films. On the surface they are very similar and Dearden achieves pretty good realistic effects on the stage at Ealing. There is a very dramatic and rather well-executed falling wall at the climax of *The Bells Go Down*, but in detail the fires are very different. During one, a fireman (Nan's husband, played by Philip Friend) with a branch on top of a turntable ladder notices a 'phone on the window sill of the burning building. He picks it up to call Nan. Such a clearly absurd action has no place in the documentary. Nor does the utterly undisciplined, constant intermingling of fire-fighters and members of their families at the scene of the blaze, which happens more than once in *The Bells Go Down*.

It is not merely a question of availability or copyright, or some other such factor, that has caused the images of fire in *Fires Were Started* to be used endlessly as 'real' or 'authentic' pictures of the Blitz, while the parallel shots in *The Bells Go Down* languish in their artificiality in the archive. This recycling is simply a measure of the 'documentary value' of *Fires Were Started*. Despite the reconstructions and inventions of both films, there is a clear difference between them and that difference can easily be termed 'documentary'.

Upon completion of principal photography, Jennings went off to Wales to begin his next assignment, *The Silent Village*, even as he and McAllister continued to edit the 'fire film' under the title *I Was a Fireman*. Trouble with this cut started early in December 1942. To Jennings' considerable shock and annoyance, *I Was a Fireman* was not well-

An authentic picture of the
blitz – Jennings burns
St. Katherine's Dock

The fire was felt to be
'particularly good'

received. That is to say, the film, Jennings wrote to Cicely, 'although adored by almost everybody did not go down well with the commercial distributors – at least that was the story. It was felt that "the picture was *much* too long and slow".'

A preview showing in Preston, Lancashire, on 4 December 1942 had produced a report claiming that 'the film was deplorably slow for the first half-hour' although the fire was felt to be 'particularly good'.

The Bells Go Down with its attractive stars *and* its claims for its own authenticity was also in the final stages of production at this time. This contributed to the MoI's worries about *I Was a Fireman*, not so much because of the history of hostility between the feature industry and the

Documentary Film Movement, or the lingering feeling that the government should not be involved with the film business at all, but simply on the grounds that the first film to reach the screen would glean all the publicity and box-office rewards.

It must be said that, although only seventy-one minutes in length, *I Was a Fireman* does take its time by dramatic norms. The three initial expository sequences and the very similar fourth 'Before Battle' sequence occupy some thirty-three minutes, nearly half the film's running time. The expositional style of editing, the detail of process – the very elements that supported the 'documentary value' of *I Was a Fireman* – were seen to weaken its effectiveness as a drama. The distributors, who were operating a voluntary rota which required them to take official productions in turn, really wanted a speedier start. In the event, Jennings and McAllister were able to compromise, re-cutting the picture but without removing any sequence wholesale. It finished up eight minutes shorter and was re-titled *Fires Were Started*.

It is often assumed that *I Was a Fireman* is nothing more than an alternative title and that the two films are the same. Ironically, given the subtlety of the re-cut, this is less of an error than it should be. Nothing significant is missing from the shortened version. It is more a question of constant trimming – losing a shot of table-tennis here, or a few synch words about fire-boats there. In this way, for example, the first three sequences are cunningly shortened from 22'45" to 17'17"; but, despite the perception that it was documentary detail holding up the narrative drive, almost all the documentary detail and the 'instructional' editing style survives – just as one might expect it would, given that the re-edit was done by two such obsessive cutting-room denizens.

Finally, on 29 March 1943, Jennings was able to tell Cicely that *Fires Were Started* 'has at last reached the screen – and (no doubt to the amazement of the timid officials in charge) has received honestly a tremendous press'. Dilys Powell in the *Sunday Times* wrote : 'The scenes, largely reconstructed, have an authenticity which is moving and terrifying, and the acting and presentation seem to me to set a new standard in this kind of documentary.' The rest of the press agreed: 'Magnificent'; 'Inspiring'; 'Thrilling'; 'Stirring'; 'a noble and convincing tribute to the firemen'. Only the *Daily Telegraph* demurred, still finding the film too slow and lacking in fires. In the *New Statesman* 'William Whitebait' (George Stonier) patiently explained how the exposition was needed to build suspense and why: 'I think [The *Telegraph*] misses the point. ... *Fires Were Started* creates its own tempo – which is quite rightly not that of the dramatic feature film – and brilliantly justifies it.'

A couple of weeks later, *The Bells Go Down* was not so well received. *The Times*:

> *The Bells Go Down* is unfortunate in that it so quickly follows the documentary film *Fires Were Started*. It is by no means true that a documentary film must, by the very virtue of its office, be better ... but here the film which was acted by men who were actually in the N.F.S. is superior at nearly every point.

Fires Were Started opened in two West End theatres. From the outset, it was received as a triumphant justification of the principles of the documentary.

9

....

'THE MURKY AND UNDECIDED REALITIES OF TODAY'

Lindsay Anderson firmly categorised all Jennings' films, including *Fires Were Started*, as documentaries; by 1954 when Anderson was writing, his concern was only that Grierson's public education strategy had forced audiences into believing the term 'documentary' to be synonymous with dull, official film-making. Since those days, the development of Direct Cinema has transformed common understanding of the documentary form. Not least because of the rhetoric of the Direct Cinema film-makers themselves, no reconstruction, however sincere and justified, has a place in documentary production any longer – supposedly. The documentary instead has bound itself to the norms of journalism and the full range of its expression is largely reduced, especially in the Anglophone world, to a strict observationalism. For the tv mainstream there is little space for poetry, personal essays, meditations, theses, re-enactments – the medium demands just flies-on-the-wall. Even David Meeker, the compiler of the Archive list, has wondered if *Fires Were Started* is 'what we would still call a documentary?' But I cannot see why not.

As I hope I have shown, I think it is possible to demonstrate the ways in which classic documentaries, however much re-enacted, can still be significantly different from fiction. I would argue that *Fires Were Started* also seems to make a good case for maintaining a distinction between the classic documentary, with all its reconstructions, and the new television genre of drama-documentaries. In his exhaustive account of the possible meanings of this term Derek Paget concludes that 'a drama-documentary will tend to use the names and identities of real historical individuals and stay close to the pattern of (relatively) verifiable real life events'. The dramadoc initially required some form of verbatim text which could be transferred to the screen using actors and sets – this requirement involved legal transcripts. The justification for this was that the original trial or inquiry could not for whatever reason be filmed. This transference then became the re-enactment of eyewitness accounts, but again with actors and sets. Such a procedure, though, rapidly approaches the conventions of our drama in general where the appearance of the 'names and identities of real historical individuals' are a commonplace. After all, there is even an historical Macbeth buried somewhere on Iona! This is not the same as real people 'acting' themselves in scenes and sets which legitimately follow a real-life pattern (as in *Fires Were Started*). This seems to me to constitute a distinction that does make a difference. The two start in significantly different places.

More than that, I am unhappy at the suggestion that only contemporary observational film-making constitutes valid documentary. Not only is this too limiting, it implies a truth-claim for the current dominant, journalistic 'fly-on-the-wall' style which is more than a little spurious. Film-makers, however much they might wish to pretend to be flies-on-the-wall, still have to tell stories. They still make un-filmed arrangements to gain access to their material. They still decide when to turn the camera on and off and what framing to use. They still edit. And, as I write, the current 'scandal' in the UK of observational documentary 'fakery' reveals the extent to which pretence that these everyday procedures do not occur leads to absurd expectations as to what truths about the real world are really on offer. I do not condone deliberate misrepresentation (of course), but the contemporary panic about 'lies', by insisting on some pretty unattainable levels of authenticity, has gone well beyond the issue of mendacity. We seem to be making quite primitive assumptions about documentary 'fakery' and the public damage caused by it – as if filming could ever entirely avoid intervention, and editing could eschew manipulation, even in the most everyday observational situations.

The assumption that the observational mode is the only way of reaching a cinematic truth is, finally, as naive as the old belief that the camera by its very nature cannot lie. In rejecting that absurdity, we inevitably make space for the 'truth' of the classic documentary, for the creatively treated actuality of *Fires Were Started*. It would be asinine to cast aside the accumulated opinion, which holds Jennings to be a master at capturing the reality of our condition, because of some simplistic, mechanistic – yet actually tendentious – view of the in-built veracity of the hand-held camcorder. The deeper truth, if you will, that was created in *Fires Were Started* remains to this day.

This 'truth' is in the barrage balloons and the T.T.L.s against the sky, the dray-horse in the fire-threatened street, the majestic Thames sailing barge; in the shy smile of the young girl in the mobile canteen; in Barrett's diffident apology to Mrs T. for arriving at 14Y a bit late; in the 'windy bastards' hitting the deck; in the 'Sorry for the interruption'; in the frantic cry, 'Get down off that bloody roof!!!'; in B.A.'s 'We mustn't work too hard, my friends. This job must last till one.' Indeed, 'This is what it was like. This is what we were like – the best of us'; and there is no reason for us to demur from the opinion of the film's first critics. As the *Daily Herald* said at the time, this documentary is 'a vivid piece of British war-time social history that speaks for itself'.

It still does.

APPENDIX: 'ONLY CONNECT:
SOME ASPECTS OF THE WORK OF HUMPHREY JENNINGS'
BY LINDSAY ANDERSON

. . . .

Reprinted from *Sight and Sound*, vol. 23 no. 4, Spring 1954

It is difficult to write anything but personally about the films of Humphrey Jennings. This is not of course to say that a full and documented account of his work in the cinema would not be of the greatest interest: anyone who undertook such a study would certainly merit our gratitude. But the sources are diffuse. Friends and colleagues would have to be sought out and questioned; poems and paintings tracked down; and, above all, the close texture of the films themselves would have to be exhaustively examined. My aim must be more modest, merely hoping to stimulate by offering some quite personal reactions, and by trying to explain why I think these pictures are so good.

Jennings' films are all documentaries, all made firmly within the framework of the British documentary movement. This fact ought not to strike a chill, for surely 'the creative interpretation of actuality' should suggest an exciting, endlessly intriguing use of the cinema; and yet it must be admitted that the overtones of the term are not immediately attractive. Indeed it comes as something of a surprise to learn that this unique and fascinating artist was from the beginning of his career in films an inside member of Grierson's G.P.O. Unit (with which he first worked in 1934), and made all his best films as official, sponsored propaganda during the second world war. His subjects were thus, at least on the surface, the common ones; yet his manner of expression was always individual, and became more and more so. It was a style that bore the closest possible relationship to his theme – to that aspect of his subjects which his particular vision caused him consistently to stress. It was, that is to say, a poetic style. In fact it might reasonably be contended that Humphrey Jennings is the only real poet the British cinema has yet produced.

II

He started directing films in 1939 (we may leave out of our account an insignificant experiment in 1935, in collaboration with Len Lye [in fact he had made 6 films before 1939]); and the date is significant, for it was the war that fertilised his talent and created the conditions in which his best work was produced. Watching one of Jennings' early pictures, *Speaking from America*, which was made to explain the workings of the transatlantic radio-telephone system, one would hardly suspect the personal qualities that characterise the pictures he was making only a short while later. There seems to have been more evidence of these in *Spare Time*, a film on the use of leisure among industrial workers: a mordant sequence of a carnival procession, drab and shoddy, in a Northern city, aroused the wrath of more orthodox documentarians, and Basil Wright has mentioned other scenes, more sympathetically shot – *'the pigeon-fancier, the 'lurcher-living collier' and the choir rehearsal are all important clues to Humphrey's development'*. Certainly such an affectionate response to simple pleasures is more characteristic of Jennings' later work than any emphasis of satire.

If there had been no war, though, could that development ever have taken place? Humphrey Jennings was never happy with narrowly propagandist subjects, any more than he was with the technical exposition of *Speaking from America*. But in wartime people become important, and observation of them is regarded in itself as a justifiable subject for filming, without any more specific 'selling angle' than their sturdiness of spirit. Happily, this was the right subject for Jennings. With Cavalcanti, Harry Watt and Pat Jackson he made *The First Days*, a picture of life on the home front in the early months of the war. On his own he then directed *Spring Offensive*, about farming and the new development of agricultural land in the Eastern counties; in 1940 he worked again with Harry Watt on *London Can Take It!*, another picture of the home front; and in 1941, with *The Heart of Britain*, he showed something of the way in which the people of Northern industrial Britain were meeting the challenge of war.

These films did their jobs well, and social historians of the future will find in them much that makes vivid the atmosphere and manners of their period. Ordinary people are sharply glimpsed in them, and the ordinary sounds that were part of the fabric of their lives reinforce the glimpses and sometimes comment on them: a lorry-load of youthful conscripts speeds down the road in blessed ignorance of the future, as a jaunty singer gives out 'We're going to hang out our washing on the Siegfried line'. In the films which Jennings made in collaboration, it is risky, of course, to draw attention too certainly to any particular feature as being his; yet here and there are images and effects which unmistakably betray his sensibility. Immense women knitting furiously for the troops; a couple of cockney mothers commenting to each other on the quietness of the streets now that the children have gone; the King and Queen unostentatiously shown inspecting the air raid damage in their own back garden. *Spring Offensive* is less sure in its touch, rather awkward in its staged conversations and rather over-elaborate in its images; *The Heart of Britain* plainly offered a subject that Jennings found more congenial. Again the sense of human contact is direct: a steel-worker discussing this A.R.P. duty with his mate, a sturdy matron of the W.V.S. looking straight at us through the camera as she touchingly describes her pride at being able to help the rescue workers, if only by serving cups of tea. And along with these plain, spontaneous encounters come telling shots of landscape and background, amplifying and reinforcing. A style, in fact, is being hammered out in these films; a style based on a peculiar intimacy of observation, a fascination with the commonplace thing or person that is significant precisely because it is commonplace, and with the whole pattern that can emerge when such commonplace, significant things and people are fitted together in the right order.

Although it is evident that the imagination at work in all these early pictures is instinctively a cinematic one, in none of them does one feel that the imagination is working with absolute freedom. All the films are accompanied by commentaries, in some cases crudely propagandist, in others serviceable and decent enough; but almost consistently these off-screen words clog and impede the progress of the picture. The images are so justly chosen, and so explicitly assembled, that there is nothing for the commentator to say. The effect – particularly if we have Jennings' later achievements in mind – is cramped. The material is there, the elements are assembled; but the fusion does not take place that alone can create the poetic whole that is greater than the sum of its parts. And then comes the last sequence of *The Heart of Britain*, the Huddersfield Choral Society rises before Malcolm Sargent, and the homely, buxom housewives, the black-coated workers, and the men from the mills burst into the 'Hallelujah Chorus'. The sound of their singing continues, and we see landscapes and noble buildings, and then a factory where bombers are being built. Back and forth go these contrasting, conjunctive images, until the music broadens out to its conclusion, the roar of engines joins in, and the bombers take off. The sequence is not a long one, and there are unfortunate intrusions from the commentator, but the effect is extraordinary, and the implications obvious. Jennings has found his style.

III

Words for Battle, Listen to Britain, Fires Were Started, A Diary for Timothy. To the enthusiast for Jennings these titles have a ring which makes it a pleasure simply to speak them, or to set them down in writing; for these are the films in which, between 1941 and 1945, we can see that completely individual style developing from tentative discovery and experiment to mature certainty. They are all films of Britain at war, and yet their feeling is never, or almost never, warlike. They are committed to the war – for all his sensibility there does not seem to have been anything of the pacifist about Jennings – but their real inspiration is pride, an unaggressive pride in the courage and doggedness of ordinary British people. Kathleen Raine, a friend of Jennings and his contemporary at Cambridge, has written: 'What counted for Humphrey was the expression, by certain people, of the ever-growing spirit of man; and, in particular, of the spirit of England.'

It is easy to see how the atmosphere of the country at war could stimulate and inspire an artist so bent. For it is at such a time that the spirit of a country becomes manifest, the sense of tradition and community sharpened as (alas) it rarely is in time of peace. 'He sought therefore for a public imagery, a public poetry.' In a country at war we are all members one of another, in a sense that is obvious to the least spiritually minded.

'Only connect'. It is surely no coincidence that Jennings chose for his writer on *A Diary for Timothy* the wise and kindly humanist who had placed that epigraph on the title page of his best novel. The phrase at any rate is apt to describe not merely the film on which Jennings worked with E.M. Forster, but this whole series of pictures which he made during the war. He had a mind that delighted in simile and the unexpected relationship. ('It was he,' wrote Grierson, 'who discovered the Louis Quinze properties of a Lyons' swiss roll.') On a deeper level, he loved to link one event with another, the past with the present, person to person. Thus the theme of *Words for Battle* is the interpretation of great poems of the past through events of the present – a somewhat artificial idea, though brilliantly executed. It is perhaps significant, though, that the film springs to a new kind of life altogether in its last sequence, as the words of Lincoln at Gettysburg are followed by the clatter of tanks driving into Parliament Square past the Lincoln statue: the sound of the tanks merges in turn into the grand music of Handel, and suddenly the camera is following a succession of men and women in uniform, striding along the pavement cheery and casual, endowed by the music, by the urgent rhythm of the cutting, and by the solemnity of what has gone before (to which we feel they are heirs) with an astonishing and breathtaking dignity, a mortal splendour.

As if taking its cue from the success of this wonderful passage, *Listen to Britain* dispenses with commentary altogether. Here the subject is simply the sights and sounds of wartime Britain over a period of some twenty-four hours. To people who have not seen the film it is difficult to describe its fascination – something quite apart from its purely nostalgic appeal to anyone who lived through those years in this country. The picture is a stylistic triumph (Jennings shared the credit with his editor, Stewart McAllister), a succession of marvellously evocative images freely linked by contrasting and complementary sounds; and yet it is not for its quality of form that one remembers it most warmly, but for the continuous sensitivity of its human regard. It is a fresh and loving eye that Jennings turns on to those Canadian soldiers, singing to an accordion to while away a long train journey; or on to that jolly factory girl singing 'Yes, my Darling Daughter' at her machine; or on to the crowded floor of the Blackpool Tower Ballroom; or the beautiful sad-faced woman who is singing 'The Ash Grove' at an ambulance station piano. Emotion in fact (it is something one often forgets) can be conveyed as unmistakably through the working of a film camera as by the manipulation of pen or paint brush. To Jennings this was a transfigured landscape, and he recorded its transfiguration on film.

The latter of these four films, *Fires Were Started* and *A Diary for Timothy*, are more ambitious in conception: the second runs for about forty minutes, and the first is a full-length 'feature-documentary'. One's opinion as to which of them is Jennings' masterpiece is likely to vary according to which of them one has most recently seen. *Fires Were Started* (made in 1942) is a story of one particular unit of the National Fire Service during one particular day and night in the middle of the London blitz: in the morning the men leave their homes and civil occupations, their taxi-cabs, newspaper shops, advertising agencies, to start their tour of duty; a new recruit arrives and is shown the ropes; warning comes in that a heavy attack is expected; night falls and the alarms begin to wail; the unit is called out to action at a riverside warehouse, where fire threatens an ammunition ship drawn up at the wharf; the fire is mastered; a man is lost; the ship sails with the morning tide. In outline it is the simplest of pictures; in treatment it is of the greatest subtlety, rightly poetic in feeling, intense with tenderness and admiration for the unassuming heroes whom it honours. Yet it is not merely the members of the unit who are given this depth and dignity of treatment. Somehow every character we see, however briefly, is made to stand out sharply and memorably in his or her own right: the brisk and cheery girl who arrives with the dawn on the site of the fire to serve tea to the men from her mobile canteen; a girl in the control room forced under her desk by a near-miss, and apologising down the telephone which she still holds in her hand as she picks herself up; two isolated aircraft-spotters watching the flames of London miles away through the darkness. No other British film made during the war, documentary or feature, achieved such a continuous and poignant truthfulness, or treated the subject of men at war with such a sense of its incidental glories and its essential tragedy.

The idea of connexion, by contrast and juxtaposition, is always present in *Fires Were Started* – never more powerfully than in the beautiful closing sequence, where the fireman's sad little funeral is intercut against the ammunition ship moving off down the river – but its general movement necessarily conforms to the basis of narrative. *A Diary for Timothy*, on the other hand, is constructed entirely to a pattern of relationships and contrasts, endlessly varying, yet each one contributing to the rounded poetic statement of the whole. It is a picture of the last year of the war, as it was lived through by people in Britain; at the start a baby, Timothy, is born, and it is to him that the film is addressed. Four representative characters are picked out (if we except Tim himself and his mother, to both of whom we periodically return): an engine driver, a farmer, a Welsh miner and a wounded fighter pilot. But the story is by no means restricted to scenes involving these; with dazzling virtuosity, linking detail by continuously striking associations of image, sound, music and comment, the film ranges freely over the life of the nation, connecting and connecting. National tragedies and personal tragedies, individual happinesses and particular beauties are woven together in a design of the utmost complexity: the miner is injured in a fall at the coal face, the fighter pilot gets better and goes back to his unit, the Arnhem strike fails, Myra Hess plays Beethoven at the National Gallery, bombs fall over Germany, and Tim yawns in his cot.

Such an apparently haphazard selection of details could mean nothing or everything. The difficulty of writing about such a film, of disengaging in the memory the particular images and sounds (sounds moreover which are constantly overlapping and mixing with each other) from the overall design has been remarked on by Dilys Powell: 'It is the general impression which remains; only with an effort do you separate the part from the whole ... the communication is always through a multitude of tiny impressions, none in isolation particularly memorable.' Only with the last point would one disagree. *A Diary for Timothy* is so tensely constructed, its progression is so swift and compulsive, its associations and implications so multifarious, that it is almost impossible, at least for the first few viewings, to catch and hold on to particular impressions. Yet the impressions themselves are rarely unmemorable, not merely for the splendid pictorial quality, but for the intimate and living observation of people, the devoted concentration on the gestures and expressions, the details of dress or behaviour that distinguish each unique human being from another. Not least among the virtues that distinguish Jennings from almost all British film-makers is his respect for personality, his freedom from the inhibitions of class-consciousness, his inability to patronise or merely to use the people in his films. Jennings' people are ends in themselves.

IV

Other films were made by Jennings during the war, and more after it, up to his tragic death in 1950; but I have chosen to concentrate on what I feel to be his best work, most valuable to us. He had his theme, which was Britain; and nothing else could stir him to quite the same response. With more conventional subjects – *The True Story of Lili Marlene*, *A Defeated People*, *The Cumberland Story* – he was obviously unhappy, and, despite his brilliance at capturing the drama of real life, the staged sequences in these films do not suggest that he would have been at ease in the direction of features. *The Silent Village* – his reconstruction of the story of Lidice in a Welsh mining village – bears this out; for all the fond simplicity with which he sets his scene, the necessary sense of conflict and suffering is missed in his over-refined, under-dramatised treatment of the essential situation. It may be maintained that Jennings' peacetime return to the theme of Britain (*The Dim Little Island* in 1949, and *Family Portrait* in 1950) produced work that can stand beside his wartime achievement, and certainly neither of these two beautifully finished films is to be dismissed. But they lack passion.

By temperament Jennings was an intellectual artist, perhaps too intellectual for the cinema. (It is interesting to find Miss Raine reporting that, 'Julian Trevelyan used to say that Humphrey's intellect was too brilliant for a painter'.) It needed the hot blast of war to warm him to passion, to quicken his symbols to emotional as well as intellectual significance. His symbols in *Family Portrait* – the Long Man of Wilmington, Beachy Head, the mythical horse of Newmarket – what do they really mean to us? Exquisitely presented though it is, the England of those films is nearer the 'This England' of the pre-war beer advertisements and Mr Castleton Knight's coronation film than to the murky and undecided realities of today. For reality, his wartime films stand alone; and they are sufficient achievement. They will last because they are true to their time, and because the depth of feeling in them can never fail to communicate itself. They will speak for us to posterity, saying: 'This is what it was like. This is what we were like – the best of us.'

NOTES

· ·

1 Grierson left the G.P.O. Film Unit in 1937, and Alberto Cavalcanti took over as producer; but Cavalcanti had joined Michael Balcon at Ealing by 1940 and Ian Dalrymple, a mainstream film editor, screenwriter and producer was appointed to run the Unit. Grierson moved to Canada and set up the National Film Board there as war broke out.

2 The surrealism of this image, or the flash of the incendiary which catches a frightened dray-horse as it is led down a street, or the inflated barrage balloon on a barge's deck, hint at the truth of the observation that in the Blitz one might well find Lautréamont's definition of surrealism – a sewing machine and an umbrella on a dissecting table – to be quite everyday.

3 Griffiths also told Vas that the local fire brigade was not alone in being unhappy with the shoot: 'We had a deputation come down with a letter about we were Fifth Columnists who were lighting up the sky for the Germans to come and bomb us. Well, that same night they come over, right, and they dropped a couple. Cos the hooters gone and I'm flying up the hill to go down the shelter and this old girl shouts out as she goes up the hill – "You'll get the bloody lot of us killed one night, you will!!"'

4 Griffiths, whom Watt considered for the part of a soldier in the Ealing production *Nine Men* also being made during this period, went on after the War to a career playing loveable Cockneys in more than 200 film and tv productions.

5 This is one reason why I think Vaughan's book so significant. It is the most sustained, considered and well-argued attack on the simplicities of the auteurist position that I know.

6 The same was true in Germany where eventually audiences were actually locked into the cinemas to make sure they watched the weekly *Deutsche Wochenshau*.

7 A somewhat elusive phrase, attributed to Grierson without citation by Forsyth Hardy in 1946, and by Rotha in 1952, but traced by Derek Paget to a 1933 article in *Cinema Journal*, a Scottish publication edited by Grierson himself.

8 Jennings' 'Bare first treatment of National Fire Service story' was headed 'THE BELLS WENT DOWN'. This document is dated 'Denham Studios, 4th January 1942'.

9 Dearden's first real box-office success was *The Captive Heart* in 1946. MacDougall later co-wrote *The Man in the White Suit*.

CREDITS

· ·

"Fires were Started –"

UK
1943
GB trade show
1 April 1943
GB release
12 April 1943
Distributor
G.F.D.

Director
Humphrey Jennings
Producer
Ian Dalrymple
Script
Humphrey Jennings
Camera
C. Pennington-Richards
Editor
Stewart McAllister
Construction
Edward Carrick
Music
William Alwyn

Production Company
Crown Film Unit
With the full co-operation
of Home Office, Ministry of
Home Security and the
National Fire Service
Production Manager
Dora Wright
Unit Manager
Nora Dawson
Production Assistant
Francis Cockburn
Story Collaborator
Maurice Richardson
Musical Director
Muir Mathieson
Assistant Editor
Jenny Stein
Construction Assistant
Loris Rey
Sound
Jock May
Recordist
Ken Cameron

Cast
Commanding Officer
George Gravett
Sub-Officer Dykes
Leading Fireman Philip
Wilson-Dickson
Section Officer Walters
Leading Fireman Fred
Griffiths
Johnny Daniels
Leading Fireman Loris
Rey
J. Rumbold, 'Colonel'
Fireman Johnny
Houghton
S.H. 'Jacko' Jackson
Fireman T.P. Smith
B.A. Brown
Fireman John Barker
Joe Vallance
Fireman William Sansom
Mike Barrett
Assistant Group Officer
Green
Mrs Townsend
Firewoman Betty Martin
Betty
Firewoman Eileen White
Eileen

Black & White
63 minutes
5,683 feet

Originally called *I Was a*
Fireman (previewed in
Preston, Lancs. on 4th
December 1942), then
shortened and retitled
"*Fires Were Started –* "
for the general theatrical
release.

Credits compiled by
Markku Salmi, BFI
Filmographic Unit

BIBLIOGRAPHY

· ·

Aldgate, Anthony, and Jeffrey Richards, *Britain Can Take It: The British Cinema in the Second World War* (Oxford: Basil Blackwell, 1986).

Anderson, Lindsay, 'Only Connect: Some Aspects of the Work of Humphrey Jennings', *Sight and Sound*, vol. 23 no 4, Spring 1954.

Bachmann, Gideon, 'The Frontiers of Realist Cinema: The Work of Ricky Leacock', *Film Culture*, vols 19–23, Summer 1961.

Barsam, Richard, *Non-Fiction Film* (New York: E.P. Dutton, 1973).

The Bells Go Down, Campaign Book, BFI Collection.

Corner, John, *The Art of Record: A Critical Introduction to Documentary* (Manchester: Manchester University Press, 1996).

Coward, Noël, *The Lyrics of Noël Coward* (London: Mandarin, 1965).

Curran, James and Vincent Porter (eds), *British Cinema History* (London: Weidenfeld, 1983).

Dalrymple, Ian, 'Personal Tribute', in *Humphrey Jennings 1907–1950*.

Documentary News Letter, no 4, 1943.

Eliot, T.S., quoted in Stedman Jones, 'The Cockney and the Nation 1780–1988'.

Elul, Jacques, *Propaganda: The Formation of Men's Attitudes* (New York: Vintage Books, 1965).

Feldman, David, and Gareth Stedman Jones (eds), *Metropolis: London Histories and Representations Since 1800* (London: Routledge, 1989).

Fires Were Started: BFI Script Collection.

Grierson, John, 'Humphrey Jennings', in *Humphrey Jennings 1907–1950*.

Harrisson, Tom, 'Film and the Home Front – The Evaluation of Their Effectiveness by "Mass Observation"', in Pronay and Spring, *Propaganda, Politics and Film 1918–1945*.

'Heart of Britain', *Omnibus*, dir. Robert Vas, BBC TV 1970. Includes interviews with Lindsay Anderson, Marius Goring, Fred Griffiths, Charlotte Jennings, Cicely Jennings, Mary-Lou Jennings, Stuart Legg.

Hillier, Jim, *The Films of Humphrey Jennings* (London: BFI Education Department, n.d.).

Hodgkinson, Anthony, 'Humphrey Jennings and Mass-Observation: A Conversation with Tom Harrisson', *Journal of the University Film Association*, vol. 27 no. 4, Fall 1975.

Hodgkinson, Anthony, and Rodney Sheratsky, *Humphrey Jennings: More than a Maker of Films* (Hanover, N.H.: University Press of New England, 1982).

Holloway, Sally, *Courage High!: A History of Firefighting in London* (London: HMSO, 1992).

Hood, Stuart, 'John Grierson and the Documentary Film Movement', in Curran and Porter, *British Cinema History*.

Humphrey Jennings 1907–1950: A Tribute (London: Humphrey Jennings Memorial Fund, nd).

Jackson, Kevin (ed.), *The Humphrey Jennings Film Reader* (London: Carcanet, 1993).

Jennings, Cicely, 'letter', *20th Century*, February 1959.

Jennings, Humphrey, *Pandæmonium*, eds Mary-Lou Jennings and Charles Madge (New York: The Free Press, 1985).

Jennings, Mary-Lou (ed.), *Humphrey Jennings: Film-Maker/Painter/Poet* (London: BFI, 1982).

Jennings Collection Item 6, BFI.

Lambert, Gavin, quoted in Millar, '"Fires Were Started"'.

Liversidge v. Anderson [1942], A.C. 206.

Manvill, Roger, 'Foreword', in Hodgkinson and Sheratsky, *Humphrey Jennings*.

Millar, Daniel, '"Fires Were Started"', *Sight and Sound*, vol. 38 no. 2, Spring 1969.

Morley, Sheridan, *A Talent to Amuse* (London: Michael Joseph, 1986).

Nichols, Bill, 'Questions of Magnitude', in John Corner (ed.), *Documentary and the Mass Media* (London: Edward Arnold, 1986).

Nichols, Bill, *Representing Reality* (Bloomington: Indiana University Press, 1991).

Paget, Derek, *No Other Way To Tell It: Dramadoc/docudrama on Television* (Manchester: Manchester University Press, 1998).

Penrose, Roland, 'Forward', in Mary-Lou Jennings (ed.), *Humphrey Jennings*.

Powell, Dilys, *Films Since 1939* (London: British Council/Longmans, Green, 1947).

Powell, Dilys, 'Films Since 1940', in *Humphrey Jennings 1907–1950*.

Pronay, Nicholas, 'The News Media at War', in Pronay and Spring, *Propaganda, Politics and Film*.

Pronay, Nicholas, and D.W. Spring (eds), *Propaganda, Politics and Film 1918–1945* (Basingstoke: Macmillan, 1982).

Randall, A.W.G., quoted in Pronay, 'The News Media at War'.

Rotha, Paul, *Rotha on the Film* (London: Faber and Faber, 1958).

Sansom, William, 'The Making of *Fires Were Started*', *Film Quarterly*, vol. 15 no. 2, Winter 1961–2.

Stead, Peter, 'The People as Stars: Feature Films as National Expression', Taylor (ed.), *Britain and the Cinema*.

Stedman Jones, Gareth, 'The Cockney and the Nation 1780-1988', in David Feldman and Gareth Stedman Jones (eds), *Metropolis: London Histories and Representations Since 1800*.

Sussex, Elizabeth, *The Rise and Fall of British Documentary* (Berkeley: University of California Press, 1975). Includes interviews with Edgar Anstey, Ian Dalrymple, Pat Jackson, Stuart Legg, Harry Watt.

Taylor, Philip (ed.), *Britain and the Cinema in the Second World War* (London: Macmillan, 1988).

Trevelyan, Julian, quoted in Anderson, 'Only Connect'.

Vaughan, Dai, *Portrait of an Invisible Man: The Working Life of Stewart McAllister, Film Editor* (London: BFI, 1983). Includes interviews with Ken Cameron, Francis Cockburn, Nora Dawson (Lee), Joe Mendoza, C. Pennington-Richards, Jenny Stein (Hutt).

War Poet, prod. Colin Moffat, BBC Radio 3, 23.12.95. Includes interviews with Denis Forman, Kevin Jackson.

Welch, David, *Propaganda and the German Cinema* (Oxford: OUP, 1983).

White, Rob, 'Degrees of Excellence' (interview with David Meeker), *360 Film Classics from the National Film and Television Archive*, *Sight and Sound* insert (London: BFI, 1998).

Winston, Brian, *Claiming the Real: The Documentary Film Revisited* (London: BFI, 1995).

ALSO PUBLISHED

If you would like further information about future BFI Film Classics or about other books on film, media and popular culture from BFI Publishing, please write to:

**BFI Film Classics
BFI Publishing
21 Stephen Street
London W1P 2LN**